Making Our Lives Work

✠ ✠ ✠

Making Our Lives Work

*Strategies to Lessen Stress
and
Build Self-Esteem*

Third Edition

✠ ✠ ✠

Shirley A. Mahood

© 1994, 1999, 2013 by Shirley A. Mahood
All rights reserved
First edition published 1994
Printed in the United States of America

ISBN 1-887322-14-0

Library of Congress Catalog Card Number: 99-72942

For additional copies of this book or to schedule a seminar, you may contact the author directly by e-mail at smahood@cox.net.

To my husband, Chuck Mahood,
whose support remains invaluable
&
To our two daughters, Diana and Wendy,
who continually help teach me what really
matters in life.

✠ ✠ ✠

Table of Contents

✠ ✠ ✠

When Our Lives Work
✠ ✠ ✠

When our lives work, we are not afraid to take away our masks, to let people see who we really are.

When our lives work, we are willing to try new things, to risk, so that we may expand and enrich our comfort zones.

When our lives work, we are so busy discovering our own talents that we don't have time to manipulate or control other people.

When our lives work, we understand that anger is only a feeling. It is right to acknowledge and then appropriately release it.

When our lives work, we pause, without judgment, when crisis hits; we allow ourselves recovery time, knowing that we are worth that effort.

When our lives work, we are comfortable in the silence of our own thoughts.

When our lives work, we realize that our ability to forgive others is hampered if we cannot forgive ourselves.

When our lives work, we use our talents for our own pleasure and for the good of the community.

When our lives work, we give ourselves the time to see where we want to go, and then we take steps to begin that journey.

When our lives work, we are able to communicate our needs, at the same time being very aware of the needs of others.

When our lives work, we live enthusiastically and radiate peace.

Shirley A. Mahood

Acknowledgements

Many people have contributed to making this revised edition possible. For all of those people who kept gently prodding me by asking when my next book was coming out, I give thanks. For all those who were willing to attend my workshops and seminars in this country and in England, I give thanks. Our collective wisdom continues to grow. For those who had patience with me while I worked on this book, I give thanks. I have indeed been blessed.

As we all make our lives work even better, let us continue to be grateful for all the kindness that can be found in our lives. And may we never forget that we have a responsibility to pass it on.

Introduction

✠ ✠ ✠

Have you been noticing that there seems to be something missing in your life? Do you have a vague sense of discontent, but perhaps for no real reason that you can identify? Are you feeling stressed? Do other people seem to be luckier or happier than you? Does it seem you never get the breaks? Each morning do you get up reluctantly and then half-heartedly begin again the same old pattern? Do you find yourself using stalling tactics rather than getting on with what needs to be done? Do you go to bed at the end of the day with little feeling of satisfaction?

For many years too much of the time I felt like that. At those times life just seemed to be a series of often boring, repetitive habits. I was not aware of how much I could do to change my life for the better. I grew up taking on much of the negative thinking that surrounds us today. When things were going well, I was worried about when they would not go well. If life was good, I didn't enjoy it completely because I was too busy imagining what "bad" things were just around the corner. I somehow felt that life was meant to be a struggle. Does this sound familiar? It doesn't matter why I felt this way or where I learned it. The reality is I did.

Then, after a childhood and young adulthood in which my life generally went well, conforming to the expected pattern – education, marriage, career – suddenly all began to come apart. Major problems surfaced in very dramatic ways. I was forced to see that my usual ways of coping were not working, and worse, I was forced to see that my expectations of life were not only unrealistic, but harmful. I was plunged, much against my own will, into a period of extreme soul searching which led to real changes not only in the way I acted, but more importantly, in the way I thought.

In the midst of all this a part of me still believed that this life is supposed to be good. As a Christian I believe the words of Jesus: I have come so that you might have life and have it abundantly (John 10:10). But I have struggled to get that abundant life, and I have watched others struggle as well. Then I began to realize that God also expected me to be involved in making my life better. I was not to be a passive receiver, but rather a person taking some proactive steps. I began by examining how I thought, and I recognized the damaging influence of negative thoughts, how they could make bad things worse and good things not so good. As I worked on those, my life did get better.

Still I often felt more tired than I wished to feel, found my temper could get very short over little things at times because physically I was pushing my body beyond its limits, and I even found that good times didn't feel as good as they should. And I see everywhere I go today, at the workshops and seminars I direct, as I listen to friends discuss how their lives are going, many are feeling the same.

Just reading books cannot change our lives, however. We have to really want to make things better, and then we have to do the mental work required, and then we have to take some positive actions. I can't make anyone take the journey to greater self-awareness, but I can tell you that the rewards you will receive are worth every struggle you may encounter.

Now I see things very differently. I learned that how my life went was largely up to me. I could choose to find it satisfying or not. This, then, is a book of hope. That is the good news. We can all make our lives better, and that means even if they are relatively good now. It takes commitment by us to do this. It means caring enough about ourselves to think first of all that we deserve to have a good life. It has not been decreed somewhere that some people deserve a better life than other people. While it is true that some people may seem at the time we are looking at their lives to be finding things much easier than we are, no one will get through life without some unhappiness, some traumatic events. That is the bad news. The good news is that we can all learn how to cope with those difficult times. And we can even learn to understand that they bring a gift of added strength and eventually joy into our lives. We won't feel that at first, we can be sure, but by following some of the guidelines in this book, we can adopt a new way of looking at life.

My first book on this topic having been written five years ago, it has become time to bring out a new edition. While all of what I had included in the original book remains, much has been added. It is my hope that you will use this book as an aid to making your lives even better than they may be at this moment. We can learn how to find and keep satisfying relationships, how to find and keep careers, whether volunteer or paid, which are satisfying. We can learn how to adopt different attitudes. The material within these pages was developed initially for use by the members of my *Making Our Lives Work* eight-week seminars. Those class members who were willing to examine their lives and risk change are finding that their lives are much more satisfying.

It is possible for our lives to work for us. When we begin to think and act in accordance with our own best interests, the world benefits because we put the best we can into that world joyously, rather than grudgingly.

What I say in this book is in no way meant to take the place of medical treatment, professional counseling, support groups, or any other form of therapy. We all have different needs, and different approaches work for us at different times. My hope is that you will find some information that helps you, that encourages you to make your life work for you.

Live Enthusiastically

Learn to find the joy in each day.

✠ ✠ ✠

Chapter One

✠ ✠ ✠

Live Enthusiastically

*When our lives work, we live enthusiastically
and radiate peace.*

Where is the joy these days? How much fun are we having? The older I get, the more I realize how very short life is, and then I ask myself why have I so often found it hard to just relax and enjoy, to feel enthusiastic? Do you know what I am talking about? I'm talking about living a life that isn't really bad, but doesn't seem too great either. I am talking about spending days in ways that make us feel like we are just getting by, rather than having mornings where we wake with enthusiasm to begin the adventure of a new day. For some readers becoming enthusiastic may seem an impossible goal. Some of us may feel that trying for such a goal is asking too much. We just want to get by, to survive. That's what life is about for us, just somehow hanging on. Trying to find joy as well is out of the question, but perhaps we need to rethink that philosophy. There are good reasons to try to find the fun, the joy, the contentment, or whatever word we might want to use to express a feeling that "all's right with the world."

3

Why is it in our best interests to become enthusiastic?

Besides enjoying a feeling of peacefulness, there are two other important reasons why it is important to live life as enthusiastically and joyfully as possible.

1. Stress is significantly reduced when we are content.

All negative thoughts find a place to reside in our bodies. For some of us it may be in our heads, constant headaches; for some of us it may be in our digestive systems; aches and pains through our bodies can be telling us that all is not well with how our lives are going. However, today's culture seems to be telling us to ignore these warning signals, just get a pill and carry on. Unfortunately, all too often that is just what we do – we ignore the messages our bodies are trying to send us. Instead of taking time to pause and look at what is happening in our lives when we have that body pain, we grab some medication and keep on going. And for a time this may work, but eventually our bodies often rebel. We may become very ill, and then, and only then for many of us, do we begin to examine what is going on in our lives, in our jobs, in our leisure time, with our relationships. We then may take the time to see what in our lives is not working, what is making us feel far from content.

Many studies have been done confirming the fact that how we are thinking and acting is indeed having an impact on our physical bodies. Any way that we can lessen the physical and emotional symptoms of stress just makes good sense. Adopting an approach of looking at the positives, of becoming more relaxed, of learning to take better physical care of ourselves, and thus becoming more enthusiastic is good for our health.

2. And not only our health benefits, but learning to live enthusiastically also brings good for the health of our world.

Only when we truly find meaning for our own lives, find the joy, will we be able to spread it in a world that sorely needs

4

it. The steady legacy of bad news that we are confronted with daily is often being caused by people who have not made their lives work for them. Because they feel angry, discontent, resentful, they need to stop other people from feeling good. It is a genuine truth that we can spread only what we have inside of us. If we are filled with anger, eventually that anger will have to be expressed. Either we will find a way to attack someone else, whether with words, with lawsuits, with physical violence, or we will attack ourselves, either physically by following very unhealthy practices, or inwardly, giving rise to depression. Negative emotions cannot remain submerged forever.

To find our own happiness, then, will make not only our lives work, but because we feel better, we will treat others better. We will not be "out to get" anyone, and we will be well enough in ourselves to find a way to make a difference. To live enthusiastically is good for us and it is good for our world. Can there be a better reason to make this our goal?

For much of my life, however, I was certainly not living life with enthusiasm, at least not most of the time. Although things did seem to be going well, I very often did not take any real pleasure in the fact that they did. I was much more taken with those things that were not going so well. And for many years those things, I see now, were relatively minor. Then everything for me changed drastically; some very difficult events happened, and I was forced to reassess nearly everything I had ever believed. And hard as that time was, it was those circumstances that freed me in a way I might never have been freed otherwise.

What is the meaning of life anyway? Why are we here? These are questions many of us ignore, being too caught up in what we have to do on a daily basis to even take time to think about them. I didn't give much thought to those questions myself until the serious difficulties of my life began to surface. And that is the problem. For too many of us, we are so busy with just getting through our days that we can forget to look at the "big picture." What is the big picture anyway?

For me the big picture is an understanding that each of our lives is a gift, one that we are to enjoy. We have been given life, a truly great gift. It is ours to treasure. Sure, some of us may not have had much in the way of nurturing in our early days, and that lack of nurturing can have a devastating impact. But it is now today. And from today we can begin to take the steps to find ways to enjoy the gift that is our life. That does not mean that we are to be selfish, to just look out for number one; it does mean, however, that we are to be thankful for our lives, to be grateful for the good things we have. If we have come to a point that the pain in our lives is outweighing the joy on a regular basis, then life is sad indeed.

Life can feel overwhelming at times. Financial concerns can cause real worry — jobs or lack of them. Fear for our own health or the health of those we care about can dampen our joy. And sudden, unexpected disasters can hit us as well. Listening to the news itself most days can certainly dampen our enthusiasm. It can be easy to be sucked into a way of thinking that tells us life is far from pleasurable; rather it is something just to be endured.

Some of us may even feel guilty if things seem to be going well for us, so we manufacture our own problems just to feel more comfortable. It can be a hard thing to acknowledge that we do this, but often we become so familiar with dealing with trouble that it just feels right. I found myself guilty of this for many years; I somehow had arrived at the belief that life was hard, and although mine wasn't especially hard at the time, I could make even the easiest things seem difficult. That's how life was supposed to be, I thought. If you enjoy life too much, eventually "the fates" will get you. So, it seemed reasonable to try not to let those "fates" think you were enjoying things too much. Instead, if I always found the not-so-good element in every situation, then I would be spared any really bad thing, I thought. Well, how wrong I was. After following that way of thinking for a number of years, some really bad things started happening to me anyway. I wish now that I had taken full enjoyment of my joys earlier. Those experiences did teach me a lot, however.

When life really did get hard, I learned that one can survive difficult times by keeping a careful eye out for the good that is also happening. And those times have given me a new sense of peace. I can now understand that yes, life can get very difficult at times, but there are always joys hiding in the midst of the pain. It is our responsibility, however, to find and enjoy them. And when things are going really well, it is our responsibility to fully enjoy those times!

For awhile when my series of troubles began, I didn't want to take on that responsibility of looking for the good, of seeing the ways that God was trying to sustain me. It can be much easier to wallow in our problems; it can even get us some benefits. People may feel sorry for us. We may get extra attention. And depending on who our friends are, we may even fit in better if we seem miserable. There are whole groups of people who enjoy finding the bad in everything. If these are our acquaintances, family members, friends, then we may feel out of place if suddenly we begin to discuss what is going on that is good.

For much of my life I had been busy raising a family, having a career, trying to feel fulfilled. The only problem was, I often didn't feel fulfilled at all. I realized that I was accomplishing many things, and I had many satisfying relationships, but something still was missing. I felt exhausted. Or, the other extreme, I felt bored. Then, suddenly, or so it seemed, my life was turned upside down by circumstances beyond my control. I was forced to question nearly everything I had always believed.

7

My cherished belief – that if you did "the right thing" you were guaranteed great results – hadn't worked. I felt I had been doing life "right," so why had it turned out like this – full of pain? I felt cheated. What's the point anyway? *What* is this life all about? Where is the satisfaction? I couldn't find the answers.

If we are to have a meaningful life, it seems to me that we must all eventually look at these questions in the light of our own experience and expectations. If someone would have told me a few years ago that I should live enthusiastically, I would have said, "You must be joking. How can I, with all this pain, with all these responsibilities, with all the uncertainties of life? There's too much that can go wrong."

Today I am changing. Today I lead workshops and seminars to help others find their own answers for more meaningful lives. The process takes time; I still don't always get it right by any means. But I am learning, with the help of those people who have been willing to share their experiences. Perhaps some of what we have learned will help you. Because I can easily slip back into non-productive ways of thinking myself, I do understand people when they tell me that it's hard to be enthusiastic when

The world's in such a mess.

The financial picture is so uncertain.

Family members are in such difficulties.

We don't feel well.

The weather is terrible.

And so on.

It's true. Life is uncertain, and very difficult at times, but we can still improve our view of our own circumstances, and in the process of doing that, very often the circumstances themselves almost magically become better. And even if they don't change, our seeing them differently means they cause us less stress. We can improve our view of our circumstances, and we need to do it. Whether we are dealing with big or little problems, the theory remains the same. When the great evening with family and friends gets canceled, we can either complain, moan, and just drift around the house, or we can think how nice it is that we have some unexpected free time and take advantage of the opportunity by doing something we usually don't have much time to do. Or when a bigger problem like serious illness, divorce, or major family difficulties arise, we can decide to dwell on how awful it all is or we can look to see how we are still being blessed by good friends, enough money to cope, or even just beautiful surroundings to enjoy. We can always find something, if we will take the time to look.

There is so much all around us to appreciate, once we take the time to look for it. Some days are hard, filled with sorrow and unhappiness. We cannot escape these times, but we can come through them. We can be open once again to all the pleasure that remains around us. Living enthusiastically is not about pretending that everything is perfect when it clearly is not. It is about learning to lessen the impact of difficult times and learning to focus on what is still good.

The saddest people are those who approach the end of their days only to look back in regret at what they did not do, or what they failed to appreciate. Those of us who are Christians can recall as well the words of Jesus when He told us that He had come so that we might have life and have it abundantly (John 10:10). Our life is meant to have joy. What I know today is that a large part of the responsibility for finding that peace and contentment is ours.

And yet, for too many years, I was so busy struggling to keep up that I never even thought about whether or not I was having an abundant life. And, as I looked around, I saw many other people in the same situation. I saw people who felt that life was not going at all as they would have wished. This feeling is best expressed by one of my class members when she said, "I've just realized I don't know what it (life) is all about. I have a reasonably good existence, no more problems than anyone else, and yet I have this nagging sense that there should be more."

How did we get stuck in our unfulfilled lives anyway?

One of the big reasons that we may be living lives that feel unfulfilling or unsatisfying is that "frantic" best describes how our days go. We get all caught up in what needs to be done and we soon find we have little, if any, time to reflect on what it is we want from this gift of life. I know just how this feels. It has taken me some time to understand that life could have so much more meaning if I began to handle things differently. As I have said, it was only when I was stopped in my tracks by situations I could not handle that I began to find the joy in everyday life. You can be sure that I did not find that joy right away, not by any means. It was a process, a step-by-step method of changing, which brought me to a much better place. I was forced to look at what I thought and how I handled things, to see which of those things worked for me, and which did not

At times it is normal and usual to feel discontent, even at times full of despair. This is part of being human, but when these periods become increasingly frequent, we need to look for the reasons. We need to look at why our minds turn so often to the negative, unhopeful ways of thinking. What we will discover is that we have gotten this way by listening to all sorts of people. We've been paying attention to what "society" thought was important. We've wanted to belong, to do it right, and so we headed down the prescribed, correct path. It didn't matter that for us a different path might be more important. Perhaps we were raised in an atmosphere of negativity. Perhaps we grew up among people who always seemed to expect the worst.

Now many of us have arrived at a place in our lives, only

to look around and wonder if it is where we want to be after all. We may keep on in our pattern, but we find very little satisfaction in it. We look with envy at others who seem to be doing just what we would like to do, who are living how we would like to live. We think they just must be the lucky ones.

Some of us do not even know that we are in pain; but pain is what it is when we feel that life is, if not totally meaningless, at least not at all satisfying. We have hidden our true emotions for so long that we don't even know that we hurt. And for those of us who recognize that we do hurt, we often blame someone else or "the situation" for that pain. Something "out there" is responsible. And so we go on living our lives, probably to the outside world even seeming to be doing a good job of it, but inside we do not feel any sense of joy, contentment, or peace.

How do we begin to change?

1. We change by taking some time to find out who we really are.

Only when we know who we are, what we like to do, what we don't like to do, what we are proficient at doing, and what we are not so skilled at doing, will we begin to know what will work for us, what will give us an abundant life. We can all have lives that are personally satisfying. It is so important that we do. But frequently we haven't taken the time to really get to know *us*. We probably have concentrated on our weaknesses and our responsibilities, but it is unlikely that we have taken the time to analyze the positive sides of our character. Even what we like to do for our own enjoyment is often more determined by other people than by us.

2. We change by learning to monitor our thought processes.

Be careful how you think; your life is shaped by your thoughts, Proverbs 4:23 tells us. And that is true. Whatever reason you may be telling yourself for your failure to feel content, it is really only one reason – your thought pattern is telling you not to. It is not the circumstances or people in your lives; it is the way you are thinking about them that is causing your unhappiness. We always have the freedom to decide what attitude we will take about any given situation. We can see all the bad or we can look for the good, even if it feels hard to find at times.

It is our mind that determines how our life goes, not the events of our life. Let me repeat: it is our mind, and not the events of our lives, that determines whether or not we find our lives satisfying. Yes, serious, sad, tragic things can happen to us, but, I repeat, it is not *what* happens, but what we *think about* what has happened that colors our days. Many of us are stuck in patterns of thought that are no longer working for us. They may have been satisfactory, as mine were, until something comes careening into our lives and upsets all our expectations.

3. We learn to not expect guaranteed results.

Because we go to the "right" university, we are not automatically guaranteed the best job. Because we send a friend a gift, we are not guaranteed a gift in return. Because we buy an expensive car, we are not guaranteed trouble-free motoring. Because we do "what is right" in any circumstance, we can not guarantee receiving the "right results."

We often tend to feel that if we play by the rules, (who makes these rules, I wonder), we will be guaranteed good results. Nothing could be further from the truth. We have no control over outcomes. No matter how "perfectly" we may be trying to run our lives, some event or person may suddenly invade our space and cause havoc. If that happens, our lives will work much better if we can learn to deal with the situation, whatever it is. Instead, many of us, as I did, spend our time either denying the seriousness of whatever has happened or complaining about how unfair it is that this should be occur-

12

ring. When we learn not to have expectations about how life should be, we can more fully enjoy the way it is.

To live enthusiastically, remember:

1. Life is a great gift. Find the joy in it daily.

2. Your thoughts, not the events or people in your life, are your real life.

Up until 1988 I only partially believed the first premise, and hadn't given a moment's thought to the second. Because my faith is important to me, I try to follow the Bible's teachings; but I came to realize that I was neglecting this very important entreaty: Love the Lord and follow . . . enthusiastically. (Joshua 22:5, TLB).

Then I was confronted with a major challenge to my expectations of how life should go. The events are not my story to tell, but my reaction is. I was thrown into a period of confusion, a period when all my expectations of right and wrong were challenged. I had played by the rules, and I didn't deserve what was happening to me, or so I thought. I said over and over, "It's not fair. I don't deserve this. I've always done the best I could." My life felt like anything but a great gift, more a series of days to get through somehow, with no expectation of ever again finding any enthusiasm.

The fact that it was my mindset that was causing much of the problem was never considered. Instead, I thought it was the circumstances alone that were making me miserable, unable to sleep, to concentrate, to enjoy any of the things I usually enjoyed. I was ready and able to see who and what was to blame. And blame I did, if not always vocally, always in my mind.

Thankfully, as I have said, I gradually began learning. In order to begin to make changes in our lives, it is necessary to begin to think differently than we may have thought before. I couldn't believe it at first, but it is true.

What would make *your* life work?

What exactly do we want from our lives? This is the step that often stops people immediately – they simply do not know. Some of us have spent so much time concerning ourselves with others in our family or with our career that we have lost sight of who we are, what skills we have that we haven't developed, even what we *really* like to do. Many of us have just been reacting to what has been happening in our lives. We have not taken the time to ask whether we are feeling content.

When, in my workshops, I ask people to say what they would do with an afternoon, or a week, or a month that they could spend any way they wish, it is always interesting to note how many people really cannot think what they would do. They have lived their lives on *have to's, should's, must's.* They don't even know what for them is fun, is joy, is bliss. I was the same for many years.

Some people take the easy way, and say, "Oh, I wish I had a million dollars, a super car, a great house or some other material thing." We all know that those things may bring joy for a time, but that is not lasting. Instead we need to consider what we individually find satisfying to do, not necessarily for any material gain. For some it is time spent playing the piano; for some it is an afternoon with a good book; for some it is painting, for some it is a long walk; what is it for you?

Invariably, people will tell me they don't have time to do what they would like to do because they *have* to do other things. But the truth is *we don't have to do anything.* It is very true that we will have to deal with consequences of our decision to do or not to do something, but we *always have choices.* We may not want a particular consequence so we don't wish to

14

make a particular choice, but we *always have choices.* Sometimes taking the consequences of an unconventional choice is healthier for us, for our well being.

You don't *have* to visit your mother-in-law every Sunday. You don't *have* to drive each of your children to activities every day after school. You don't *have* to keep talking on the phone to someone who regularly interrupts your day with unimportant chat. You don't *have* to take over the leadership of any committee just because no one else seems to be going to do it. What will happen if you don't?

Exercise: Write down what you would do if you could have your own perfect day — one in which you could do anything you wanted to do — no difficulty with expense, the only criteria being you had to do it by yourself. (Your day might include people once you got to a place, say an antique market, if that were your choice, but you must go on your own.)

This exercise should be showing you something about yourself. Are you seeing that being alone is a big issue? Are you seeing that you don't even know what you really want to do? Those are two good reasons why we fail to enjoy our lives, why we are not living enthusiastically. We may feel we need someone else to do an activity with us, and if no one else can join us, we don't do the activity either. This is particularly true of women. And, secondly, if we don't know what we like to do, how can we possibly have the pleasure of enjoying that activity?

Exercise: Write down the activities you did in the past week that were enjoyable to you. How much of your week was taken up with those activities?

This exercise often shows us how little time we spend doing what we like to do; is it any wonder then that we are not finding life very satisfying? Oh, I know, all those responsibilities. Sometimes we need to look more carefully at those responsibilities, to see just which ones are really ours and which perhaps are not. Are we doing too much for some people who need to be doing more for themselves? Are we overlooking the fact that when one person in a group, whether in a family or in a work place, is doing too much, someone else is not doing enough?

It is true that some of us so need to feel needed that we take on jobs that should be someone else's. It isn't good for us, and, more importantly, it isn't good for the person who is not doing his share. This is how dependent people are created. Helping one another is a good thing, but taking over and doing for them is not. (More about this in chapter four on control)

We always can find time for what we really want to do. We just sometimes have to convince ourselves that it is important that we also have "play" time, and not just "work" time. We may need to remind ourselves that life is not all about work. God gave us gifts to use for other people, but also just for us to enjoy ourselves. Sometimes deep, almost unconscious thoughts are preventing us from being able to let go and enjoy. When this is the case, therapy can be a very beneficial tool.

Some readers may be feeling quite uncomfortable right now with the thoughts that come to mind if you genuinely considered those two exercises. It remains contrary to popular thinking for so many that life is meant to be fun. For many it is just a struggle day in and day out, but it doesn't have to be. *We can make our lives better.*

Why this emphasis on self, someone always asks in my workshops. The reason again is this: we can only spread enthusiasm if we feel enthusiastic. The world sorely needs an injection of this type of thinking; we can help start the process.

To live enthusiastically is the only way to live.

We can learn to fully appreciate each of our days, regardless of what is going on around us. Because some of us often get stuck in believing we don't really deserve a good life, we intentionally and unintentionally sabotage ourselves, thereby insuring that we don't get it. We say, "Oh yes, taking up painting, which I was really good at in school, would be fun, but I have no money or no time or a sick relative or . . ." We forget that problems can be solved; people can become willing to help us seek our dream.

"But life is full of pain," you repeat. "How do you expect me to live enthusiastically?" Life is indeed often full of pain, but we can survive pain, and then we can really appreciate the joy. After a particularly painful time for my family, I remember saying to a friend when discussing this concept of joy: When you have been through hell, joy is everywhere. I think it is true, but we must seek it out. We must accept and feel all the pain and then we can go ahead to our enthusiastic life. (More about his in chapter six on crisis.) For now, just keep an open mind about your right to an enthusiastic life. No one is any more deserving than you.

Self-Esteem

Give yourself a break.
Perfection is not a requirement.

✦ ✦ ✦

Chapter Two

✠ ✠ ✠

Self-Esteem

When our lives work, we are not afraid to take away our masks to let people see who we really are.

O
ne of the major stresses of our lives is caused by our need to hide who we are from other people. We do it in big and in little ways. Not giving our opinion but instead taking the position that we think everyone else has, only going places other people choose because we are afraid our choice will not be accepted, and choosing our material possessions based on current fads are just three examples of how we hide our true selves behind a mask. Instead of letting people know what we think or where we like to go or what we like to wear or own, we instead try to figure out what is the acceptable response. Why do we do this? We do it because we are afraid that we won't be liked if we let others see what we think. We may have developed a strong "people pleasing" attitude. While it is good to like to support people when we can, it is not good to lose our personal identity in the process. When we can stop trying to impress people, when we can stop trying to figure out what they want from us and then stop trying to give it to them when it is not in our best interests to do so, we will feel such

freedom. It will mean that we don't always have to stop and analyze every word and every action to try to determine what someone else will think about it. We can learn to be ourselves.

Of course, there is an important element here: one of the reasons we may be afraid to shed our masks is because we really don't like ourselves very much. We may have unrealistic expectations of who we "should be." We may think we need to be perfect or at least try to show others a perfect self. We may feel we won't be respected otherwise. If this is the case, then we can be very afraid of letting anyone see the "real us." For much of life that described me. I so wanted people to like me that I hesitated doing anything that I thought might in any way offend them. As a result, I woke up one day realizing that I had nearly forgotten who I was. I had lost "me" in my attempt to please everyone else. The mask I wore was becoming concrete, a heavy burden to say the least.

Eventually I learned the truth in this statement: It is impossible to make our lives work if we don't like ourselves. Think about that for a minute. Do you like yourself? Lots of us are guilty of so often finding fault with the things that we say and do that eventually we begin to think of ourselves as lacking all the positive qualities we see in other people. Perhaps other people in our lives have helped us to feel this way. Parents, teachers, and other authority figures often unknowingly do a lot of damage to self-esteem by the way they treat us and the words they use when they speak to us. They compare us to our brothers and sisters, even our cousins; they tell us we are *always* late, *always* irresponsible, for example, falsely assuming this will give us incentive to improve. Mostly it gives us the incentive to prove them right, to our detriment.

Try this test: On a scale of 1 to 10, with 10 being the goal, how much do you like yourself? Take the time to think about this. Be honest with yourself. Ideally, we should all be in the

8–10 range. Were you? Why are we so hard on ourselves? Why do we think we have to do and say everything perfectly? We are human beings, after all, and humans are far from being perfect. Because we often are so critical of ourselves, we don't feel like we are worthy of that good life, that enthusiastic life that we were talking about in the last chapter. That's for other people, those people who "have it all together."

The truth, of course, is that no one has it all together all of the time, no one. As individuals we each have the same amount of value; we have different skills, but we all matter. When we consistently put ourselves down, we set ourselves up for an unhappy, unfulfilled life. All of us have the potential to improve. People *can* change. Constantly we are learning how to do things differently. If we keep an open mind, there will always be more to learn. We will never be finished and perfect in this life, but so what? At least let's learn to appreciate ourselves now, to value ourselves, to pat ourselves on the back when we do something well, and to learn from those things we don't do so well at first. Let's not give up on ourselves.

Jesus told the world: Love your neighbor as you love yourself (Luke 10:27). The last few words in that sentence are key: *As You Love Yourself.* We are to love ourselves. Many of us have taken on the first part of that sentence, the "love your neighbor," but we have failed to see the whole picture. Jesus put those last few words there for a reason. The reason is this: When we treat ourselves well, not better than we treat others, but well, we then become much less judgmental. When we make fewer demands on ourselves, we make fewer demands on others. We allow for imperfections, both in ourselves and in others. How well do you love yourself? And if you are loving your neighbor as you love yourself, will this be good for your neighbor?

This is such an important concept that it needs to be stressed more than once. In order to love other people we have to first love ourselves. How do you treat someone you love? With patience, with concern, with caring. Do we treat ourselves the same way? Not often enough. Instead we may get very busy doing for others all the time, trying to make ourselves feel good. We may be trying to make up for all the wrong things we think we have done. But we have gotten things in the wrong order. Doing for others does make us feel good temporarily, but if we don't feel good in ourselves, the old self-hate crops up again and so we have to get busy and do some more "good works." What usually happens is that we become exhausted, and then we can give to no one. Doing things to help others is important, but it must be done with the right motivation, our sincere caring, not our need to feel better about ourselves. When we give to ourselves first, when we learn to value ourselves, as Jesus told us, we then have the energy to give to others.

Who are you letting define you?

Let's look more closely at where we get our sense of ourselves, our self-esteem. Whenever I ask this question in my workshops, the answer is always the same: from other people. Why do we let other people tell us who we are, what we are good at, or what we are not so good at? How can they possibly know us better than we know ourselves? And yet from our earliest days we have accepted the words of parents, teachers, friends, brothers, sisters, and any other people we come in contact with as being correct about what kind of people we are.

If a teacher told us we would never be good students, we believed it, or if a parent said we were lazy, we believed it, or if a spouse said we were ungrateful, we believed it. Hopefully, we were sometimes also given positive messages, but unfortunately, it seems that the positive ones are much more likely to be forgotten as we focus on the negative ones.

Let us now define ourselves.

As adults it is time to look at ourselves honestly, by ourselves, to make our own assessment of who we are. Try these exercises as a springboard to discovering those positive skills and qualities you may have been denying in yourself.

Exercise:

1. Make a list of the skills you have. Skills, as I am defining them, are those things you enjoy doing. They might be things you get recognition from, but they don't need to be.

2. Make a list of the personality traits you admire about yourself. These might include, for example, patience, sense of humor, good listener, compassionate.

How hard was this for you to do? For some people it is very hard at first. Some of us have been given negative messages for so long that it is hard to think that we have any skills or qualities that are worth while. Another problem that comes up is the problem of comparison. All of us can do many things, but we don't list them as skills or qualities because we can always think of someone else who is more expert than we. This is a major source of low self-esteem, always comparing ourselves to other people. The truth is there will always be someone who is "better" at what we do. But the greater truth is that it doesn't matter. We only have to be good enough to enjoy it. That's all there is. If I enjoy working with ceramics, then I should do it; it doesn't matter if my pieces are the best or not. If I enjoy making them, that is reason enough for finding the time to do so.

Until we begin to assess our strong points accurately, and begin to value ourselves, it will be impossible to make our lives work.

Many people do make changes, constantly, but they are often not changes that are good for them; they are led by the values and ideas of others, of society, of friends, of family. Karen,* a member of one of my most recent workshops, is just such an example. Every committee she has served on, she had joined because a friend was also a member. She admitted that she had never really considered whether or not she actually *wanted* to be on that particular committee. Her need to not disappoint her friend took precedence over her own desires. At times it can be appropriate to forget our wishes in order to help someone, but each situation needs to be assessed. When we learn to listen to our "inner voice," we will always find the right answer. The problem is that many of us have forgotten all about our inner knowing. We react to what is happening, rather than taking the time to think through the situation to determine our response. How do we hear this inner voice, some people ask. We hear it with our feelings. We hear it when we stay quiet long enough to determine how we feel about something. But too often we do not have enough quiet time in our lives to determine how we feel. It's important to find the time to examine our feelings. And when we do, if we find that resentment is the overpowering feeling, then we can be sure that our inner voice is telling us to look at this situation again.

The next obstacle may then flare up. We may now understand that we do not wish to do what we previously would have agreed to do without regard for our own desires. Karen found herself in this place. Now comes the scary part for some of us. We are going to have to confront someone to tell that person that we don't want to do something. For some of us this can be so frightening that we decide to bury our resentful feeling and pretend to ourselves that we are ok with the situation. Each time we give in, our inner voice becomes harder and harder to

*All names have been changed.

hear. Like any part of us, the more we use it, the better it works. We will look more closely at how to communicate our needs in chapter ten. For right now it is most important to understand that failing to consider our needs is a sign of low self-esteem, a sign that we don't think we matter as much as other people. Nothing could be further from the truth.

When we begin to look closely at our lives, at the activities of our days and the friends we have, it can be a daunting task. In some cases we may find that not much of what we do can we really say we enjoy. And, of course, it is not possible to always do just exactly what one wants, but we do have a great deal of control over how our lives go, as long as we take the opportunity to exercise it! Think about all the people currently following careers that their parents told them would be good for them. Some of those people are now suffering real emotional problems because they followed someone else's idea of what they should do, instead of doing what they really wanted to do. It takes time to get in touch with our feelings and to look at our lives, but it is necessary, and we are worth that time.

No one knows better than we ourselves what we need. Again, the Bible supports this belief. In 1 Corinthians 2:11 we are told that it is only a person's own spirit that knows all about him. Yet, too often we are afraid to trust our own instincts, afraid that we may be wrong. And what if we do make a few mistakes? What if we try some things that don't work out? At least we will know that we tried. No one can give us self-esteem, except us. And no one can live life enthusiastically if he is living a life according to someone else's guidelines.

Besides learning how to let our feelings guide us, we can begin to talk to ourselves differently. We can stop playing back the tapes that we have heard from other people about how we are or what we should do. We can begin our own new tapes. We can pay attention to the messages we are sending ourselves.

We can begin to make some positive changes. We can use affirmations to remind ourselves of our value. Affirmations are positive sentences which tell us where we want to be in a certain situation and pattern of thinking. For example, if managing money has been a problem for us, instead of thinking to ourselves, "Well, I've never been good at managing money," we can now begin to tell ourselves, "I'm getting better every day at managing my money." The value of doing this type of talking to ourselves really works. Whatever you feel you have not done too well in the past, you can change by making up a positive affirmation telling yourself, in the present tense, that you are doing it well. We can direct our brain to think, and thus act, differently by the words we allow it to hear.

When we hear criticism in other's words, as we will, we can learn to evaluate honestly what has been said, and if there is truth in it, we can seek to correct our behavior. But because we may need to make some changes does not mean that we have been failures up to that point. We just haven't been as good as we are now getting. And if there is no truth in whatever was said, we can learn to not accept the criticism.

When we get even stronger, we can learn to tell our critics politely it is not helpful for us to be talked to in that manner. Sometimes we can't do this at first — and that is ok. But a real sign of our strength is when we can, without anger, simply and calmly tell another person that we do not wish to be treated in a way that is damaging.

Please note: This advice, of course, is only possible when there is no history of physical or sexual violence. If violence is a feature of a relationship, a safe haven from that threat has to be found immediately.

Often the people who are saying things that hurt us and lower our self-esteem are really unaware of the damage that their words are causing. Therefore, it is up to us to tell them. When a friend of mine said something in a group that was hurtful about me, I didn't say anything at the time. But later, and actually, it was several weeks later before I got up the nerve to do it, I invited her in for a coffee, and I just said, "Probably you didn't realize it, but it was hurtful to me when you said . . ."

She immediately said she was sorry, and our friendship continues. However, I have learned that I am more careful about what I say to her because I now realize that sometimes in her pain, she uses her words to hurt others. And often this is exactly why people say things that are hurtful. It is because they are feeling hurt, in pain, themselves. Our mouths speak what our hearts are full of, another Biblical principle from Matthew 12:34.

What happens when we don't confront people who are hurting us with their words is that we come to dread being around them, and we may even start to avoid them, thereby perhaps sacrificing a relationship that could go on. And even if the relationship does not continue, we owe it to ourselves not to accept bad behavior from anyone. We are worth being treated well. We don't need people in our lives who are constantly putting us down. When these people are members of our family, it is even more important to try to work out the situation by honest, but sensitive, talk. Thousands of people live in families where one member is not talking to another. This is sad. Often it has come about because a person was hurt and no conciliatory communication followed.

We can see to it that fewer critical comments come our way by choosing our friends carefully and by learning to communicate when we are hurt, instead of withdrawing. And we can learn to talk positively to ourselves. When we hear our inner voice telling us that we can't make that announcement for our community group because we are no good at public speaking, we can stop that thought and put in a new one. We can decide that we will give it a try, maybe first getting some tips from someone with more experience.

Students in my eight-week classes have begun art classes, taken counseling courses, become leaders on committee groups, changed jobs – even careers – and joined all manner of recreational organizations. What is so remarkable about this is that each one said he or she would have not had the confidence to make these changes without learning to think differently. Before that change in thinking, they had spent their lives listening to all the negative messages around them, believing they could never do what secretly they yearned to do.

Driving along a road outside London, I saw a billboard with a great philosophy: Can't is a four letter word. Our self-esteem grows as we tackle things that we find hard to tackle, things which instead of saying we can't handle, we learn to call challenges. Every time we do something that is difficult, we increase our confidence; we increase our feeling of good will about ourselves. And if we don't do it perfectly the first or second or third time, we can feel good that we are still trying and getting better each time.

Feeling good about ourselves is vital. It is vital because it gives us the courage to make changes we need to make. It makes us realize that we have value and thus should not be treated poorly by *anyone*. It is impossible to live enthusiastically if we have people in our lives who are treating us badly on a regular basis.

Tips on how to increase your self-esteem:

1. Continually remind yourself of the positives in your life.

Look at the good things and be grateful for them. Often when we are feeling sorry for ourselves, we deliberately choose to ignore all the good that is in our lives. If we have enough to eat and a roof over our heads, those are two big reasons to be grateful right there.

Exercise: List every good thing that happened in the past week.

Surprising, isn't it? How often we focus on everything that has gone wrong, and we fail to see all that is going right.

2. Tell yourself that the things that need to be changed can be changed, and that you can do it.

Keep reminding yourself that you have just as much ability to make positive changes in your life as anyone else. You just have to start. Being willing is the first step.

Exercise: List at least one new thing you are going to do that you have until this time been reluctant and fearful to try. It doesn't have to be a big thing; it might just be a phone call you've been putting off out of fear of the reaction you might get. It might be offering to help do something that you've always wanted to do, but were afraid to try.

3. Surround yourself with positive people.

When we begin to want to feel better about ourselves, we may suddenly notice that the people around us are negative, always looking at the pessimistic side of things. We need to find those who will share our positive energy. Some of those negative people may become converted themselves, but if not, perhaps we need to begin gradually to limit the amount of time we spend with them. It is important that we explain how we are feeling, however, to give them a chance to change.

Exercise: *List the people currently in your life who make you feel good. These are the people with whom you need to spend more time.*

4. Monitor your thoughts. What are you thinking at any moment? You can change it.

As you hear yourself saying anything negative, listen and then put in the opposing positive thought. For example, if you are trying to lose weight, instead of saying, "Oh, it is hopeless anyway, so I might as well have this cake," learn to say, "No, it is not hopeless unless I choose to let it be. I am strong enough to do this."

Exercise: *For one morning or afternoon, note the negative thoughts, on paper, as they pop into your mind, and then, right next to them on the paper, replace them with positive ones*

5. Give up the idea of perfection.

This is hard because many of us have been taught so much about standards, about particular ways of doing things, but life is too short to quibble over unimportant details.

Exercise: *What do you most want your family and friends to remember you for? Sobering thought, isn't it? I doubt it's going to be for the cleanest house, or the most perfect wardrobe, or having earned the most money.*

6. Continually remind yourself that your self-esteem does not rest on how well the lives of your spouse or children are going.

Exercise: *Try to take a measure of how much time you spend thinking of the problems of family members. You probably will be surprised to see how much time is taken up in this way, time you could be spending on your own life. It is true that we must be responsive to the genuine needs of others; sometimes we can help them. It is important, however, to stop wasting our time trying to "fix" another person's life. Each adult person is ultimately responsible for his own life.*

This is often a reason for low self-esteem. We hold ourselves responsible for everyone else's happiness. *We cannot make anyone else happy.* The best spouse or parent in the world cannot guarantee another's happiness. Happiness is an individual matter. It's now time to believe in ourselves. Sure, we are not perfect, but then neither is anyone else. And people who try to pretend they are perfect don't have many real friends. Who can measure up to their standards? It's time to take off the mask and let the world see who we really are. It's time for *us* to see who we really are. Probably we have spent enough time already on our imperfections. So, we have them. We can always work on changing them, but we won't ever get it entirely right, and that is all right. What's most important is that we learn to value ourselves. The time is now.

Worry and Fear

*Worry and fear
are twin enemies we can tame.*

✠ ✠ ✠

Chapter Three

✠ ✠ ✠

Worry and Fear

When our lives work, we are willing to try new things,
to risk, so that we may expand and enrich our comfort zones.

E ven when our attitude is basically optimistic, even when
we feel generally all right in ourselves, we still at times
may feel that our lives are missing something. It happens
to all of us on occasion. We then may decide to take some time
to examine our lives, using some of the techniques from the
previous chapter perhaps. We decide what we want, we may
even take preliminary steps toward the goal, but then we come
to a dead halt. What stops us? Take the case of Mary, a woman
in one of my workshops, who had wanted for a number of
years to learn to play the piano. She even got so far as to ring
an instructor, only to be told she would have to go on a waiting
list. Eventually, she was notified that there was an opening. Her
reply to the instructor: "Well, I have gotten busier since I called,
and I can't fit it in my schedule right now."

What had happened? Yes, she genuinely had become busier.
But she was honest enough with herself, and with us, when she
admitted that though indeed she does have less time, the real
reason she didn't sign on for the lessons was fear. It was worry
that she would not be good enough and fear that she wouldn't

be able to live with that possible "failure." While she waited to be contacted, those twin enemies had time to take over.

Worry is what we do when we feel fear.

Worry keeps us from moving forward. We consider doing something; then we fear it won't work out well or other people won't like what we do – they may criticize our results, and so we worry. All the time spent worrying does not accomplish anything. Thus, we don't get on with our plan.

And not only do we not get on with our plan, worrying is exhausting. It drains us mentally and physically so our days can become just hours to be endured until we can find some rest. In days gone by life was lived on a much more physical level. Keeping ourselves fed and clothed and under a roof took a great deal of actual physical labor. Today a few professions are still very physical in nature, but most of us have so many labor-saving devices that we should indeed be well rested and able to enjoy life. However, the abundance of self-help books and support groups tells a different story. We may not be tired from working with our bodies, but we are indeed tired from listening to our own self-talk, our talk to ourselves about fear. Or we are exhausted because we keep ourselves very busy, busy enough so that we can't hear our voice of fear. If we want our lives to work for us, we need to get a grip on worry and fear.

Honestly recognizing our feelings is the first important step that we must take before we can learn to deal with our reluctance to do things.

Once we recognize our honest feelings, we can then begin to change them. When we refuse to look at the real reasons we are choosing, or not choosing to do things, we stay locked in fear. You hear these statements all the time: "I would sign up for that class, but I don't like to go out at night." Translated that means, "I don't really want to go to that class enough to overcome my fear of driving alone at night."

Or, "I'd love to travel to Asia, but I just can't get enough time off to make it worthwhile." The person who said that to me finally did admit that it wasn't about the time off. It was fear of the long plane journey.

What makes this avoiding of the real issue so detrimental is not only that we cannot begin to overcome a fear that we don't acknowledge, but also we confuse and often irritate friends. They listen to the words we are saying, and they try to help us solve that problem. They tell us how we could get more time, or more money, or whatever to do what we are not doing. They, then, of course, are surprised, and also annoyed, when we take no notice of their advice. Of course, we take no notice of it because that wasn't the real problem. The real problem was fear.

Some of us may have a dream, perhaps of becoming a successful singer, painter, designer, entrepreneur of some sort. We fantasize about it. We may tell other people about this dream. If they are good listeners, and not "rain on our parade" type people, they may ask us why we don't do whatever it is that we have said we want to do. Many of us reply that we don't have enough money or time to do it. Actually, there is great truth in the statement that when we really want to do something we find a way. And when we don't, we find an excuse. A friend of mine who often said that she wanted to concentrate more on the crafts that she did so well, perhaps eventually being able to work on commission, finally admitted that fear of not being good enough stopped her from working with all her energy toward that goal. Previously she had always blamed the fact that she was a mother with several children. Now she was being honest with herself, recognizing that she could begin, as soon as she was able to let go of the fear of failure. *It is looking straight at our fear that makes it diminish.*

Exercise: What is making you fearful right now? It's best if you take paper and pencil and actually note those things you fear. Items on the list will probably vary from some very serious things like losing a job, being ill, death, end of a relationship, child in trouble, and then go on to include fear of driving on the highway, fear of going out after dark, fear of public speaking, and so on. Use as much time as you need to think of the things that worry you.

Now with the list in front of you, put each item into one of three categories.

1. Those things which you can't do anything about.

First and foremost what goes into this category is everything that another person does. We cannot control other people, so it follows that we cannot control what they do. They may, on occasion, take our advice, but just as often, they may not. These people, including our spouses, children, brothers, sisters, parents, neighbors, and friends, may do many things which are worrying to us. We can't stop them, short of locking them up in a room with us twenty-four hours a day. And all the time we spend worrying about them is time we could more profitably be spending working on our own lives. I've said it before, but it is so important it needs to be said again: *Each adult person needs to take responsibility for his or her own life.* We need to support when we can, but then we need to get on with our own issues, giving everyone else that same privilege.

Most of the problems we read about in the news, we can do nothing about either. We cannot make countries stop fighting with each other. We cannot find solutions to the major health problems of the times. We cannot clear up the crime problem. We cannot make the management of any organization behave in a moral, ethical way.

This does not mean that we close our eyes to the whole world; we can note what is going on, and perhaps we can find some ways in specific instances to protect ourselves from the illness, crime, and poor management we read about. Perhaps we can also find productive ways to help. But worrying about how bad the times are doesn't change a thing. It only keeps us from getting on with our lives. And it keeps us from looking at all the good that is also a part of every day. It can keep us mired in negative, unenthusiastic thinking.

2. *Those things which you can't do anything about right now.*

This may include things that can be dealt with tomorrow, or next week, or next month, or next year, but not now, not today. Maybe you have just received a bill which is definitely wrong; you have been overcharged. You have opened it Friday at 6:00 pm. The office involved is now closed. There is no point in spending the entire weekend worrying about this financial error. Monday morning you can do something about it, but not now. In situations like that, we can learn to put aside that concern until the time comes that we can take some action on it. We can use positive affirmations, saying things like, "I will be able to easily deal with this situation on Monday."

Sometimes when we have a project that we need to have done by a particular time, we spend more time worrying about it, at times when we can't work on it, than actually doing it. I've gotten wiser in this regard myself. It used to be that when I had an important talk to give, I would spend many hours worrying about what I was going to say and when I was going to get around to doing the preparation. Now when I have a presentation to prepare, I decide how far ahead I need to begin work on it, and then I forget about it. I stick to my plan and begin on the appointed day. Planning puts me in charge, and feeling on top of it all takes away the fear.

41

3. Those things which we can do something about.

This, obviously, is the category that should get our attention. But too often it doesn't because we allow our minds to become too preoccupied with the other two. What's the result? You know, as well as I know. We fail to act on the things that we actually can influence.

So often we get into a pattern of inertia, based on our thought patterns – thought patterns that destroy our ability to get the things done that we can actually do at any given time. The amount of time we spend dwelling on those things over which we have no control is time we could be spending much more profitably. So it is important to take the time to look at our concerns, to determine which of those we can do something about and then to begin taking some action on those things.

Worry is good for only one thing.

Worry that becomes concern and eventually action has its place. If we realize that a big tax bill is coming in six weeks, and we are worried about it, there is some action we can take. Depending on our circumstances, we can try different ways to save money, look into installment paying, or possibly come up with an unconventional, but thoroughly satisfactory, other solution. The point is there is something we can do about that worry.

The acid test for worry:

1. Can we do anything about it now?

2. Can we do anything about it at all?

It is true that life sometimes can present us with very difficult situations, with people and events that can initially cause us a great deal of worry and concern. And it is perfectly natural to

42

feel worried for awhile. When our lives work, we become able to differentiate those worries that can lead us to action and those which just steal our valuable time.

Suppose you are very concerned about losing your job. That may be a real, and certainly serious, fear. How do you react? There are several possibilities. You could adopt the ostrich position, bury your head in the sand, pretend there's no problem. That is not what is meant by overcoming fear. We have to be realistic. You could go into work panic-stricken every day, just waiting for the ax to fall. Your nervous state would undoubtedly influence your productivity, ultimately perhaps forcing just the scenario you fear, loss of a job. You could continue doing your work, but also take time in your leisure hours to upgrade your résumé in preparation for a job search. You could begin to evaluate your financial picture to see exactly how you stand. You might have some investing choices you could make.

The same is true about anything which we fear and which we do have some control over. If it is a relationship that is not working well, instead of just worrying about what might happen, we can begin to take some action. Perhaps we take some time to assess how to communicate in a more helpful manner. Perhaps we look at what our role is in this situation, what we could do differently instead of spending time blaming the other person. It always takes two people to keep or destroy a relationship. One may seem to be more the cause of the problem, but the second person's response can either help or hinder the situation. Worry is significantly reduced when we begin to take some steps to do something. The something we do may in fact just be learning to think differently about what might happen.

Concern which leads to action is highly beneficial. Just worrying and doing nothing leads nowhere. Losing a job today often falls into category one, something that we cannot do anything about. We may not be able to keep our job, but we can

43

do some things to get ready for that possible eventuality. We may not be able to keep a certain relationship, but we can at least learn to think differently about the outcome, and who knows, as we change our thinking, the relationship might be saved. If it has deteriorated into a blaming game, then our decision to step out of that game could start a whole new pattern to develop a much healthier one.

Too often what happens, however, is that people caught in these positions just keep waiting, and worrying, and hoping. All that waiting, worrying, and hoping. with no action, will seldom change the outcome.

Why are we afraid to act?

We are afraid of the consequences. We want things to stay the same, even as foolish as it sounds, things we may not like very well. This is because "the devil we know is better than the devil we don't." How many times we make deliberate choices to stay in bad situations rather than going for better ones! We don't want to move out of our comfort zone, that boundary within which we feel comfortable. Every time we move out of our comfort zone we have to give up something; we suffer a loss. And loss is never easy. A new job means we have to leave the old job; a new relationship means we will probably have less time for other relationships. Even a new hobby means that we will be managing our time in a different way, having to give up something, even if that something was just extra free time. Moving out of that comfort zone takes courage.

Often what we do as we contemplate change is suddenly to see the situation in a much more positive light than we had seen it before; now as we think of changing it, we may realize it has a lot more possibilities than we had previously seen. This can be a good thing, can help us stop complaining. However, it can also be a not so good thing if it stops us from making a change that we do need to make in order to have our lives improve. It's important to look realistically at this thought pattern. Is it our genuine feeling or a reaction to fear of change?

Another reason that we can be afraid to take the necessary actions to change our lives is that we are afraid of the possibility of what we see as failure. Though we know intellectually that the only failure is the failure to try, in practice we don't want to be the one who had not accomplished what he hoped. We may even find it easy to be sympathetic to others who don't succeed. We may encourage and support them; still we don't want to be them. We don't ever want to be seen as not accomplishing what we set out to do. We all know what the result of that is. We do nothing new.

As a result we stay in careers and in relationships which are no longer working for us because we are too fearful of change and the chance of failing. How many times have you heard people complain and complain about their jobs, and yet when it is suggested that they look for a new one, they always have an answer as to why they can't. When we adopt this type of behavior in our lives, when we allow worry and fear to stop us from making changes, then we sabotage our own chance for a better life. We, therefore, don't have the abundant life we have been promised because of our own reluctance to make choices that would work for us. Then we get angry with God for not giving us the good life. He can't give us what we won't take.

There are some tips that we can use to try to extend our comfort zones. These ideas can help us make conscious decisions about those things that we can do something about and those that we might just as well stop worrying about because the eventual results will not be up to us.

Tips for extending our comfort zones:

1. We need to remind ourselves that we really have only today to deal with.

45

Oh, yes, we fill our calendars with plans for days far in advance in some cases, but no one knows exactly how life will go. The best thing to do is just to concern ourselves with making today as good as we can make it. This, of course, means there is no advantage in wasting it worrying over what we can do nothing about.

It's such a simple concept, in theory, and yet so hard to follow in practice. When we concentrate only on today, without worrying about what tomorrow will bring, we can be fully involved and enthusiastic about whatever we are doing. What happens usually, however, is that part of each day is spoiled as we spend time analyzing what *might* be going to happen in the future. That means that while we may be doing things we enjoy, a part of our mind is not taking it all in, not enjoying it because we are choosing to focus on something we fear.

How many times I used to spend weekends being only partially present in whatever was going on. I was only partially present because part of my mind was busy worrying about some upcoming event the next week. Have you also been guilty of this? And often the thing that I was so concerned about never came to pass anyway, or it was so much less a problem than I had anticipated

This looking into the future with fear of what *could* happen was responsible for stopping me from having a life that worked for me. How much more pleasure I find in each day now that I let each day be sufficient unto itself. Energy that could be spent in positive ways is less often used up by worry and fear.

Some people fail to live in the present moment because they are still focusing on the past. Past events are just that – past. We can't go back and redo them. Perhaps there are some things we can do to make a bad situation better. If we feel we have wronged someone, we can apologize. If we can no longer apologize to the person, there are other ways in which we can help ease our consciences. Christians know the value of prayer in such situations, coming to God and telling him our concern, asking for forgiveness. Some of us expect such perfection of ourselves that we can be beating ourselves up about something we did "wrong" for years after the event. That is a sure way to miss out on abundant living. Live in the moment, and let the past be past, and the future take care of itself.

2. We need to consider how important whatever we are worried about is anyway.

Does it really matter in the long run? Some things are serious and need for us to take some action in order to deal with them. However, so much of what we worry about is so unimportant in the long run, in the big picture. One of the biggest things many of us worry about in some form is that old "what will people think" adage. We worry about what people think of the job we have, the education we have, the house we live in, the way we spend our money, what our children do – the list could go on and on. What kind of impression we are making on other people does matter to a certain extent, but the people that matter base their impression of us on *how we treat them,* not on how we or our possessions look or how much success we or our family members have achieved.

Many of us have old, out-dated expectations of how things *should* be. We may feel that everyone else is judging us to see if we conform to the *standards*. It is important to have some standards in life, of course. But it is important to look at the real priorities of life. Too often we have worried so much about what "the neighbors would think" that we have kept ourselves from trying something new. The woman who feared how her piano playing would be judged is such an example. Instead of looking forward to just playing for the enjoyment of it, what others would think of her skill stopped her from taking the lessons. What matters most, her happiness or what they *might* think?

3. We need to be brave enough to look straight at our fear.

Only when we look clearly at our fear can we begin to determine how we will cope if what we fear actually happens. Doing this will accomplish two things. First it will help us see if it is even important. So much of what we worry about, as we have said, has to do with how other people will view us – our appearance, the things we do, or the things we have. We all know we can never please everyone, but a lot of us seem to want to give it a try.

But secondly, if the worry does have real justification, such as serious illness, loss of relationship, major financial implications, then looking straight at it will help us to see what action can be taken to alleviate the situation at least somewhat. We can then move from immobilizing worry into active concern. We can plot a plan and begin on it. By doing something, we immediately take back some control of the situation, and we become less fearful. Fear is nearly always based on the feeling that we have no control over the situation.

This is a topic I know a great deal about because as I look back on my life now, I see how often I made a judgment about what to do based on fear. My fears were based either on what someone else would think of what I was going to do, or fear for my safety. Well, I see now how often God was trying to give me something, which I was choosing not to accept out of fear because the gift would have forced me out of some aspect of my comfort zone. Trust in God is the supreme reliever of fear, but even people of faith at times need to stop and look again at their faith. Usually we can find some area of our lives where our trust is weaker, where we still feel fear, despite our faith.

Some people say that all our decisions are either based on fear or on faith. Well, that is really something to consider. All decisions are based on fear or on faith. That means whether we will do that announcement for our community group or not – allowing for whether we may have a previous engagement or not – is based on fear or on faith. Fear if we won't, faith if we do. Even when we may turn down an opportunity because we say we have no time, is that really true, or is it that villain fear once again rearing its ugly head? But, as I have said, we need to take time to look at the decisions we make to determine this. We can so easily try to convince ourselves that there really is a good reason why we are not doing something, instead of the reason really being fear.

How many of us have said that we don't want to try scuba diving because we don't have the time, or perhaps we won't take bridge lessons because of lack of time, or the lessons are on the wrong night? Often what we are really saying is that fear is motivating us. It isn't lack of time; it is lack of faith. One person I know frequently tells people she wishes she could travel more, but she doesn't have the money. And yet she continually spends money on upgrading a house which really does not need upgrading. The truth of the matter, she does admit at times, is that while she would love to see new places, she feels uneasy and anxious when she leaves her home.

Or consider the woman who said she wanted to take one of my workshops, but she said she didn't have the money to do so. The church she was attending told her they would pay for her to take the course. You can probably guess what happened. She still didn't take the class. While I cannot prove it, I think she really did not want to take the series, but since several people she knew were taking it, she felt she had to express an interest in doing so also. However, all she did was frustrate the people of the church who voted to give her the money which she chose not to use. Her example shows us why it is so important to know why we are making our decisions. It would have been so much better if she would have just said that she didn't want to take the course. Instead by taking the view she thought she should have, no one won, she least of all. Faith would have given her the courage to express her true feelings. Fear inconvenienced several people.

49

Worry and fear are twin enemies that prevent us from being all that God has meant each of us to be. Our lives are *our* lives. Despite the hardships that may happen, what a truly wonderful gift they are. Learning to trust, learning not to become immobilized by fear, makes an abundant life possible.

Control

Whose business are we minding?

✠ ✠ ✠

Chapter Four

✠ ✠ ✠

Control

When our lives work,
we are too busy discovering our own talent
to manipulate and control other people.

Wanting to be in charge of our lives is a universal trait. We may not want to be a leader in an organization, but we want to feel that we have some say in the events of our own lives. No one likes to feel that he has no control over his life. No one likes always to be told what or how to do something. We don't like to feel that we have no choices. We all want to be managers in some area of our lives, even those of us who do take special pleasure in helping others. We may enjoy helping, but we still don't want to feel obligated to help. When we feel that way, resentment soon builds up. And we would like some choice in how we serve. Take me, for example; I do not like to serve by being on committees. I serve with much more enthusiasm in other ways. Some people may want to serve by providing food to people in need; some may want to serve by giving of their physical skills, donating many hours to community projects. Some may want to serve by being good listeners. The point is that even in our giving, we know how we want to give. And this is fine. It is good that we know those things which we do well enough to volunteer.

We feel better in ourselves when we're doing that which we are comfortable doing. We feel better, and work with a better attitude if we have had some control in our choice of giving. The same is true of our work life; we give the best when we are at one with the job, when it is really "us." If all of us did only those things which really suited our personalities and skills, the world would certainly benefit. There would be fewer mediocre results. There would be less absenteeism as well. We tend to get to those places that we want to go to, whether those places are for volunteer or paid activities.

It only makes sense to be as much in control of our lives as possible. Of course, ultimately, only God is in charge, but He expects us to use the skills He has given us to make the best possible contribution. Are we using our best skills, or are we being busy doing that which does not really suit us? And if we are spending much of our time doing things which really do not suit us, why is that so? Is it because we have allowed other people to dictate our choices? Refer back to chapter two on self-esteem.

Besides looking at our own lives to see who is influencing our choices, who is taking control away from us, it is also important to look at how we are trying to control other people. And, when we are honest, we will find that all of us do this, some of us to a much larger degree than others, but we all do it. Think of the ways that we try to convince people to do something when we are pretty sure that they really don't want to do it. That is an example of attempting to control the behavior of another. We may do it for what we consider to be very good reasons, but we are still trying to control. All the conversations family members have regarding diets and smoking are just two examples of one or more persons trying to change the habits of another.

Control becomes a problem when we put our focus on what other people should be doing, instead of on what we should be doing.

It is tempting to do this. Adults tend to think they know what is best for other adults. Parents tend to think they know what is best for their children. As a result as parents we may try to push our children, even coerce them, into doing things our way. This is damaging for two reasons. First, what we are so sure is best for them might not be best actually. We cannot predict the future. Secondly, we will certainly severely test, if not completely destroy, any chance for a satisfying relationship.

Take this example, for instance: Pete would like to breed tropical fish. He has wanted to do so for some time but, he has not felt financially able to until recently. Naturally this project would also take time, but his teenage son is having difficulties in school, with his grades. So, each night Pete and his son sit and go over homework. Their relationship is worsening because his son, understandably, feels he is being treated like a child, and Pete usually loses his temper at least once each night.

Pete is not different from many parents in this regard, wanting to "help" their children get better grades or do better in sports or whatever. The problem is that until Pete's son *himself wants* to get better grades, no amount of time spent on homework will matter. Pete cannot *make* his son get better grades, and, more importantly, he is damaging their relationship by his overbearing behavior.

Pete's worry is about what will eventually happen to his son if he doesn't make good grades. This projection into the future of what *might* happen is destroying today. Each person, I will repeat it yet again, ultimately must run his own life. Yes, we can offer advice, but then we must let other people get on with doing things their way – even if we would not agree with their choices. We can put in some safeguards if what they are doing will potentially cause us trouble, but we cannot really ever make someone do what he or she does not want to do. If people take our advice, it is because they have decided that it matters to them to do it. For example, in the situation with Pete and his son, Pete might put in some consequences regarding his son's grades. He may say that there will be a reward of some sort for good grades, and then let his son decide what to do. Many times what is causing this concern over grades has to do so much with the future, with worry over the future. A good relationship with our children is much more important than any future "prize." And besides, we can not ever really know what the future will look like.

This is an incredibly hard thing to do, to let others be responsible for themselves. It is hard because we are so sure that we know what is best for them, and sometimes we are even right, but it is not up to us to try to *force* anyone to do, or not do, anything. We worry about what will happen to those we care about if they don't take our advice. But there is no guarantee our advice is right. It might be right for us, or for some, but that does not mean it is right for the person we want to take it. When I was in university, for example, I was not encouraged to take public speaking; people told me I could never make a living doing it. Well, today I do earn money doing just that. Other people are not always right about what we should be doing. And even if they are right, unless the person being given the advice himself wants to take that advice, it either will not be taken at all or be taken very half-heartedly. I will talk more about that later in this chapter.

If Peter stopped his so-called helping each night, he would have the time to spend developing his own interest in tropical fish. He would be happier in himself, and thus he would be easier to be around. He and his son could have a much better relationship.

What do you want out of life?

When I ask people in my workshops what they want out of life, here is one of the answers I always get — I just want everyone in my family to be happy. While that indeed is a noble idea, it is also impossible for one person to make happen. Each person in a family is responsible for his own happiness. And because our sense of ourselves, our self-esteem, cannot be conditional on how our family or friends are doing, we need to learn to stop trying to control these other people. We need to stop trying to control them *even* if it is for their own good. We need to live our lives and let other people live theirs.

But while we might easily say that we agree with that idea in theory, nevertheless, many of us spend much of our time trying to get people to act in a certain way, both for our benefit and also because we are sure that they will be happier, if they only do it our way. We are trying to control. We probably don't call it that; we say we are doing it for "their own good." But who are we to say what "their own good" is? Each of us has to find that for ourselves.

That does not mean we become anti-social and live in a cave somewhere, pleasing only ourselves. It means that we spend time developing our lives so that we have something to give to others, something we can give with joy. We all dislike those people who try to make us do things a certain way, and yet we become the same. Many of us spend much of our time trying to get people to do just what we have decided is best for them because we are sure that they will be happier, if they only do it our way. When we do this, we are trying to control them, no matter how good our intentions may be.

Life works when we get out of the way.

Other people usually become much more cooperative when we stop nagging them to be the way we want them to be. How may of us can identify with this scenario between Carol and Dan? Carol wants several household repairs done; she has tried every technique she can think of to encourage Dan to do them. Months have gone by, and nothing has been fixed.

She thinks, "If only he would change, would take an interest in the house." See those key words: *If only he would change.* That is the problem right there. We can never make anyone else change. They may change at any time, but we can not *make* them change.

What is the solution then? If Dan will not do the repairs, something else has to happen. The possibilities are many. Carol could decide to learn how to do these repairs herself, if she had an interest in that area. They could hire someone to do them, or they could decide they aren't that necessary after all. Each family would have to determine its own answers, but the key requirement is to cause no lasting damage to the relationship. And one other possibility exists: once Carol stopped nagging, Dan might take it upon himself to do some of them on his own. So many of us become perverse when we are told to do something. I have one friend who admits that even if she might have wanted to do a particular thing, once she is told to do it, she suddenly doesn't want to do it at all, and I can identify with that feeling myself!

Relationships matter most.

Whether we are talking about children, spouses, other family members, or friends, the most important thing is the quality of the relationship. It is sad to see how often relationships suffer because someone wants to control someone else. It is such a subtle thing at times. It can take the guise of being helpful, of being caring, and yet each time we try to manipulate someone into doing a particular thing, we are guilty of trying to control that individual.

Much of what we are trying to influence is not necessary in the whole scheme of life anyway. We are told that the greatest commandment, the rule of all rules on how we should treat people, is that we should love one another. We are to treat others as we would like to be treated. (Matthew 7:12). It is not loving to try to force other people to be just as we want them to be. Is our love conditional on how they behave?

Do we only love others when they do as we say? And how important are some of these rules anyway? What does it matter a month from now if a particular bedroom is clean on a particular Saturday? Or a week from now what does it matter if we put pressure on a family member to set the table in a certain way for a certain group of friends? What does it matter if a co-worker doesn't use *your* method if the work is done as requested on time?

We have so many ideas of how things should be. We know what clothes others should wear; we know how much exercise they should have; we know what food they should eat; we know they should stop harmful habits, and how they should stop them, and when; we know how people should manage their finances. We know so much about what other people should do. How are we managing our own lives when we are spending so much time trying to manage someone else's?

One of my daughters said a very wise thing which I think of often, "If you have warned me once, that is enough. You are off the hook. It is up to me whether or not I take that advice." How true, and yet how frequently we seem to keep repeating the same words, thinking that the more people hear it, the more likely they are to act. Often, just the opposite is true.

Exercise: In the past two weeks how have you tried to control other people, tried to get them to do things your way? What was the result? Was it worth the effort? Was it even that important?

Who's really in control?

Some people reading this chapter may feel that this is not about them at all. In fact, someone else may be trying to control them, not the other way around. Do you feel like this? Are you usually on the receiving end, being told how to polish the car correctly, how to furnish the kitchen, or perhaps what to say at a company gathering? What is your reaction to these comments?

Often the reaction is subtly *not* to follow them exactly – to appear on the surface perhaps to be going along, but really to somehow "forget" just part of the advice, or to delay so long that someone else has to take over. This is called passive aggressive behavior, and it happens whenever someone pretends to agree, but actually will in some way sabotage the result. It is control also, but less obvious. And it happens all the time.

Like me, I imagine you have heard people say things like, "Well, I got even with him: he wanted me to do such and such, and I did, but not like he wanted it done." Or, "I got even later by doing . . ." Many times people will agree to do something, but a lot of time goes by and the something never gets done. One person said to me that this described her husband perfectly. He never disagreed when she asked him to do a household job, but she learned after numerous times, he had no intention of doing it. Eventually she just stopped asking – he had won by using passive aggressive techniques. No one likes to be controlled. No one. It makes us feel inferior, like we don't know enough to do things right. We get defensive, and we may even try to get even. By doing so, we get a bit of the control back again. The person trying to get us to do things his way doesn't really succeed.

The trouble with passive aggressive behavior is that it never really addresses the problem. We need to learn how to communicate our needs. We need to learn how to speak up for ourselves in honest ways. The person wanting to control us needs to see that what he is doing is not helpful. Relationships in which one person always has the power don't work for either party. But dictators cannot be dictators without our cooperation.

Because I am usually organized, a "let's get on with it" type of person, for many years I felt that that was the only way to be. Therefore, it just followed that I tried to get the people I cared most about, the members of my family, to be the same. You can imagine the result. I thought I was being helpful when I told family members how something should be done. I thought I was being helpful when I reminded them of appointments; I was saving them embarrassment, I thought. What I was doing was trying to exert control. I didn't see it that way. I saw it as helping them to have happier and more productive lives. By my actions I was denying them the right to make their own decisions and make their own mistakes.

Two things I was failing to see: One, I'm not always organized by any means. At times I can procrastinate with the best of the procrastinators. Actually the revised edition of this book is a case in point. I had been going to do this for many months before I actually began it. Two, I had no right to try to influence my family to become like me. Aside from cautioning about some of society's dangers, we do not have the right to try to impose our way of doing things on others.

Parents get into control games with their children, and spouses get into control games with each other, friends get into control games; controlling personalities tend to attract passive aggressive people. The degree to which the one tries to control the other determines the degree of passive aggressive behavior.

How do we get out of this destructive pattern?

One person in the partnership has to recognize what is going on and want to change that pattern. It can be either party. In my situation I was lucky enough to have some family members who got strong enough in themselves to begin to politely tell me when I was being less than helpful. The comment I have mentioned by my daughter was a starting point.

Then when I was trying to give my other daughter advice about something that was really none of my business, her words pulled me up short. She said, "I hear you, Mom, but I'm not going to do it." These words reminded me that she is her own person. It is not up to me to run her life. I was proud of her courage, her being honest. And I was proud of how she said it, in a very light-hearted and non-threatening manner. I reminded myself that I might not always be around; how was I helping her or anyone to learn to manage for themselves if I insisted on telling them exactly how to do everything.

Then I began remembering how I had felt when other people tried to get me to do things their way. I can still hear my mother saying to me, "No one can tell you anything. You have to do it your way." Well, if I wanted to do things my way, I finally realized, so did other people.

But the lightning bolt which really caused me to modify my behavior was the realization that if I didn't have to spend so much time watching over everyone else's life, I could actually get on with my own! There were several things, like Pete, that I wanted to do, but I couldn't find the time. Suddenly, as I allowed others to run their own live, I could run mine!

Exercise: Which role are you playing most often? Are you the passive person or the controller? We may play different roles with different people.

Exercise: *What do you need to do to make these relationships more equal, more enriching? Take some time to look at this. Is self-esteem an issue? Are communication skills the problem?*

Controlling behavior is insidious. It sneaks into relationship so easily, especially when one person for a time may need extra help through a difficult period. Suddenly, we may wake up to see that we are in a very unequal relationship. We may be the one who is in danger of taking over too many responsibilities which are really not ours, or we could be the one who is having too much done for us, or too much advice given us.

We need to examine our lives to see what we need to do to change the status quo. It is no good waiting for the other person to change. We have to do the changing. The other person may or may not change, but we can learn to not be so affected. If we are the passive people, we must learn to speak up directly and honestly about what we think, and what we will do. If we are the controlling people, we need to stop focusing on everyone else and start looking at our own lives.

Exercise: *List some of your non-career activities. How many of those are still bringing you satisfaction?*

Exercise: *If you have any that are not now satisfying, why are you still doing them?*

The answer we often find to that question is that we don't want to let someone down. Here is another example of a place where control is the issue. We, in fact, are being controlled, not by what we want, but by another person. Yes, it is true that we must consider carefully the consequences when we wish to give up something, and we should give appropriate notice. But it is also true that when we do things out of a sense of being controlled, it is not good for us. It's not good for others either because we don't give our best.

Two final principles of control:

1. *The controlling personality often is that way because he does not want to look at his own life.*

He is afraid of what he might see. He is afraid to see his fears, his weaknesses, his regrets. It is much easier to focus on everyone else. I know for awhile that was my issue. There were things I wanted to do, but I was afraid to risk, to step out to do them. Instead I kept a close eye on what other people were doing and was usually ready to offer advice that was not really needed or appreciated.

2. *The person who feels controlled needs more self-esteem.*

The person who is allowing others to control him believes that others matter more than he does. He is not strong enough to stand up for himself, to demand respect.

We develop these characteristics as a result of what has happened to us in our lifetimes. It is often helpful to examine the events of our past. It is helpful to learn from them, but today is today. Now it is up to us to develop satisfying, enriching relationship based on equality.

Anger

It can help us to heal.

✠ ✠ ✠

Chapter Five

✝✝✝

Anger

When our lives work, we understand anger is only a feeling. It is right to acknowledge and then appropriately release it.

By now it is becoming very apparent that making our lives work is not easy. It takes having the courage to look carefully at ourselves. For some of us this is too frightening to contemplate. We are afraid of what we may see. It is all right to have these feelings at first. It is natural. However, if we want to find our way to enthusiastic living, it is necessary to spend time with ourselves, to spend time honestly evaluating our lives to this point. Christians should have no fear of this, realizing that all of our weaknesses, our failings, can be forgiven by God. We can then let go of those things and get on with making our lives better. Eventually, we will all see the answers that we, as individuals, need to see. When we begin to look at new ways of thinking, we may find that we feel unsure, off balance. We have held certain views for so long that changing them is scary.

This chapter is about anger. Anger is a powerful emotion. It cannot be ignored, and yet we must be extremely careful how we express it. Many of us have been taught that to get angry is not good, that we are showing a bad side of ourselves if we ever give way to angry feelings. So, each time that we are angry, we may feel guilty as well. It is time to realize that feeling and expressing anger is necessary at times. We have many tools to make our lives easier, and learning how to handle anger effectively is one of them.

Jesus, who set the perfect example of how human lives should be lived, at times got angry. There is such a thing as "righteous anger." This is anger that motivates us to make some positive changes. In nations all over the world much legislation and many support groups have been begun by people who got angry at unjust situations, people who decided to try to do something to help. Out of their anger and pain, they found ways to improve some aspect of life. But they had to control their initial, often overpowering, passion in order to accomplish their goals.

It is, of course, true that committing violent acts against a person or damaging someone's property is not an appropriate way of dealing with anger. It is also not all right to speak in degrading ways to people. As we will discuss later, we can confront people, but not in destructive ways. We must not set out deliberately to hurt another, but we can feel angry. Again, it is how we express anger that is the important issue. And, in fact, *not* expressing anger in the long run can be very destructive.

Why is it important to express our anger?

1. Keeping our anger buried inside us is damaging to our physical and emotional health.

Physically, when resentment builds up, it begins to interfere with the normal functioning of our bodies. More and more studies are showing how negative emotions impact on us physically. We get ill more often, whether we suffer backaches, stomachaches, or headaches, or we may develop emotional illnesses. Whether our body hurts or our peace of mind is shattered, the result is we don't feel well. Our physical body is telling us what our spirit is feeling —not good. For an excellent in-depth study of this concept, I recommend Dr. Bernie Siegel's book *Love, Medicine, Miracles* which explores this topic in great depth.

2. *Anger and resentment that are not expressed, which are repressed for a long time, are often unleashed with great violence.*

Newspapers report crimes where eyewitnesses say it seemed like this nice, quiet person just suddenly snapped and went on a shooting spree. We read of incidents where passive spouses, abused day after day, one day just attack and kill their mates. It is not possible to keep anger from showing up somewhere, either in our own bodies or by violent acts in society.

Today one of the current ways we are frequently seeing anger expressed is by what we have labeled road rage, abusive language and actions against a driver who is seen to have committed some driving error that upsets another. In some extreme cases drivers have even used guns when they have felt that someone got in their way. The excessive number of these incidents is showing us how many people today are far from happy with their lives; their anger is certainly showing in a most inappropriate manner.

We cannot continually pretend we are not upset. Life does not always go perfectly. Individuals and groups of people do things that bring out our anger. Perhaps we are living lives that are really not of our own choosing. Perhaps we feel that we have lost control of our own lives as we discussed in the previous chapter. Whatever the reason, when we are angry we are in pain. Eventually we have to deal with the pain.

Exercise: *Allow two or three minutes to write down everything you can think of that makes you angry.*

What kinds of things have you listed? If you are like many who have taken my workshops, your list might look something like this: unethical government officials, drivers who cut in front of you, a current local issue, family member who doesn't cooperate, or the recession.

Note that several of those items are things that you can do nothing about. Anger over things that we can do nothing about is as unproductive as worry over things that we can do nothing about. Sometimes, as in the case of worry, we concentrate on these "false" issues to keep from looking at what is really upsetting us.

What are we really angry about?

You may know of a person who always complains about everything at work, in the community, in the world at large. People like that can often go on at great length about what should be done by the "powers that be." They are indeed expressing anger, but they are masking their real anger. They do not want to see its true source. Perhaps they are actually upset with themselves and how they handled something; perhaps they are angry with a family member, and they have unrealistic expectations of what family life is all about. They think we must always be in perfect accord with each other.

This is especially true when we are angry about a situation with other people that they really have no choice about either – maybe financial or health problems that they can not control. When we don't want to see the real source of our wrath, we may choose to express it somewhere else. Instead of directing our fury at its true cause, we choose to direct it where we think it is *acceptable*.

If this happens, we often get a reputation as a complainer. And the sad thing is, we never get to the root of our anger, and we never learn to face it and go on. In fact some psychologists say that denial of anger is one of the major reasons people find it hard to get on with life. Their normal coping mechanisms shut down because they are so preoccupied with their hidden fury.

Many family gatherings have been spoiled by a family member who has to find fault with everything. When we find ourselves in such a situation, it can be very helpful to step back and consider why this person is acting that way. Remember that the mouth speaks what the heart is full of. Why is this person so angry? It is probably not at all about what he is actually blaming. The person who finds fault with other people, with how they are handling things is not at home in his own life. He is masking his anger about his own situation by finding fault with other things.

What about hidden anger?

Some people, however, don't appear to be angry. They are not the loud complaining types. Still they can be full of hidden anger. Often we hear people complaining that life is just blah, that nothing much seems worth while. These are people in the early stages of anger denial. Some of us have been told that "nice" people don't get angry. And so, when anything happens which is upsetting to us, we pretend it doesn't really matter. We pretend that we are not angry. We try to rationalize the pain away. We may become sad, rather than angry. Sadness is often a mask for anger that we feel afraid to express, perhaps because we feel it is unacceptable anger.

The trouble with this theory is that if we don't allow our angry feelings, soon we will not have any positive feelings either. We can become locked in sadness, in hopelessness, in a total lack of enthusiasm. Our lives do not go along on an even keel, day after day, and neither should our emotions. It is natural to have ups and downs. When we deny the downs, the

71

energy required to hold back those feelings restrains us from having any ups. If this goes on long enough, as we have said, physical or serious emotional conditions will result. "Nice" people do get angry, but they channel their anger appropriately.

Our minds have to be clear so that we can think logically and develop plans for our lives, for effective relationships and meaningful careers or volunteer activities. When we are trying to operate with only part of our mind because the other part is trying to overcome angry feelings, it is obvious that our thinking will be much less effective. Think of a simple example. For me I know how my emotional state is any given day by watching how I perform the simplest tasks. How many times do I forget what I have gone into a room to get? Or I may put the milk in the cupboard instead of the refrigerator. And those are just two of the strange things I may do!

Well, if my mind is constantly in that state, either through worry or anger, you can see how ineffective my life will soon become. And that is why, besides learning to deal with worry, we must learn to deal with anger so that we can make the best use of this wonderful gift that we have been given – our lives.

Exercise: Now, again list some things in your own life that you are upset about – just things in your own life.

Was this hard to do? For many it is because we have been so conditioned to think that it is not all right to be angry. We don't feel peaceful, but we refuse to think that we have anything to be upset about. We rationalize that the situation isn't anyone's fault, so how can we be angry? Or we think we should be able to rise above anger – only weak, ineffectual people get angry. Or we may have spent so little time even thinking about our lives, that we haven't considered how we feel. Or we may feel guilty because when we look around, we have things so much better than others; how dare we feel angry? Well, the truth of the matter is that if we feel angry, then we feel angry. There is not right or wrong with feelings. They just are; they just happen. Learning how to deal with them is what matters.

Anger is a very real emotion, and learning to conquer it and move on brings great rewards. It won't be easy at first, especially because some of us may have to overcome many years of being told that feeling furious is wrong. As we have said, changing how we think about things can be very challenging. It is again a loss, a giving up of ideas that once seemed to be right. Here are four tips that can help us to do just that.

Tips for coping with anger:

1. We must be very brave.

We must be ready to look at what exactly is making us angry. And we have to be honest about it. For two periods of my life I have lived outside my own country. It has been a blessing in many ways, but it has also been difficult at times. Being separated from family and friends and missing one's own culture at times made me feel angry that financial considerations made this necessary.

At first I felt guilty every time I started to feel unhappy because everyone keep saying how lucky we were, what a great experience to live in a different culture. And that is true, but at times I still did find life difficult. Any of you reading this book who have lived outside your own culture will know, I'm sure, what I mean. Yet there were so many positives, it seemed unacceptable, ungrateful to have any negative feelings about the situation. Finally, I remembered that anger is a feeling, and feelings are not right or wrong; they are just feelings. I was entitled to my feelings. I was allowed to sometimes feel angry.

That example is not as difficult as ones in which our anger is directed toward a person, especially a person who perhaps is

73

already suffering. It is easy to get very upset when we must nurse a sick relative for an extended period of time, or when financial reversals of our partner impact on us, or when a family member is going through a tough time for any reason and is taking out his frustration on us.

We may deny our anger because we think it is not fair to be angry with someone who is already in pain. Sometimes a close friend or family member has died, and we can't allow ourselves to be angry under those circumstances. It may not be reasonable, but when it is the truth, we must accept, regardless of the fairness of it, that we are angry.

So, the first step in dealing with our anger is to understand that it is ok to feel this way. And when we can allow ourselves to see that we are angry, and to see what exactly is making us angry, only then can we begin the process of overcoming that anger. As long as we pretend we are not angry or we direct our anger at something other than the real thing which is upsetting us, we will stay stuck in our pain.

2. We must find a way to vent the anger in a non-damaging way.

This is easier than it may at first appear. Talking about it is the best way, but one has to be careful with whom one talks. It is not appropriate at first to try to talk to the person who is making you so upset. Instead find someone else you can trust, a good friend or a trained counselor. The person you choose must be willing to listen without becoming judgmental; you must feel free to say whatever you need to say. If you are going to use a good friend, be sure this person is indeed a good friend. This type of friend needs to be one who can be trusted with confidential material. This type of friend needs to be one who will not try to solve your problem for you, but will just listen. This type of friend needs to be one who will allow you to have your feelings, not try to change them for you.

Unfortunately, too many friends, thinking that they are

doing the right thing, try to talk us out of our feelings. When I was feeling really angry at one point, I remember a good friend saying, "Well, you shouldn't be upset. Look at the good side of this." In that sentence she effectively told me that my feeling was not acceptable. She is a caring person, who thought she was helping me. She was not. Other people don't like to see us in pain and so out of their own need for us to feel good, they may try to encourage us to give up our negative feelings too soon. Ideally, after we have had the opportunity to express all the negativity, we ourselves can then come to the more optimistic feeling, but not until we have been allowed to express all the hurt.

After that experience I learned to choose friends to confide in more carefully. Now when I have family situations that still push my buttons, I am lucky enough to have good friends who will listen without judging me. In turn I listen to them. But it takes time to develop this type of trust.

If you don't have that type of friend right now, be on the lookout for people whom you think you could eventually trust. A valued friend is worth his weight in gold. Conventional wisdom through the generations has recognized that talking about a trouble halves it, and yet in today's world we seem to be separating ourselves from each other.

We have become so busy trying to appear perfect that we won't let anyone see when we are having trouble. And because we hide our problems, our friends are afraid to show theirs as well. We put on our "perfect lives" masks. The first result is that we can't be helped. The second result is that we can't help anyone else, since they haven't let us know they need help. Solutions are probably just around the corner, but they'll never be found as long as we persist in pretending that everything is always going well.

If neither a counselor nor a sensitive friend is available, sit down and list everything that is making you angry. Don't worry about how it sounds; it is how you feel. Then either hide this letter where no one can find it or tear it up, but you will feel better for having gotten the feelings out of you. It sounds strange but it works. Today psychologists are completing studies which indicate that those people who write out the traumatic events in their lives actually are physically more healthy than those who do not. Pain and hurt take up residence in our bodies. We need to help them to leave.

Exercise is a method often recommended for venting angry feelings, and it has value. Whatever type of exercise is chosen will relieve the physical aggressive feelings for a time. But until we get to the heart of what is causing us to feel the way we are feeling, the aggressive, "let's get them" tendencies will just keep recurring. Talking to another and writing down our thoughts help us to clarify what exactly is making us be so unpeaceful.

3. *Eventually, when you have calmed down sufficiently, it may be necessary to confront people in regard to their behavior.*

This should be done only after a cooling-down period. Chapter ten will discuss ways of confronting in a positive, non-aggressive manner. The manner of confrontation is crucial.

Too often when someone hurts us, we get angry, but we never tell the other person how he or she has upset us. When this happens, it is much harder to get rid of the anger. We may think we have forgotten the situation, but usually we have not; it is lying in wait. Then when we are hurt again, we put the next hurt on top of the previous one. Eventually, we may have several layers of hurt, all ones we think we have gotten over. Soon we become much less trusting of people. To avoid that build-up of resentment, we may need to confront the person who has caused us the pain. But it must be done with extreme care.

4. *We must stop feeling guilty for having angry feelings.*

I know this is much easier said than done. Being in a quiet

place works for me when I am trying to forgive myself, to rid myself of guilt over angry feelings. Some people go for walks; others listen to soothing music, or maybe work in their gardens. The point is we must quiet our minds, confront our anger and then recognize that we are not bad people because we have been, and perhaps still are, angry.

It isn't easy, but it can be done. After all, where is it written that we as human beings have to be perfect? We are not perfect. Christians know that the greatest gift of our faith is the fact that we can be forgiven. We don't have to live mired in guilt. God made us as creatures with emotions, happy, glad ones, but also unhappy, sad, angry ones. It is not possible to deny the opposites.

5. It is important to learn to be patient with ourselves.

Once we begin to allow ourselves to feel our angry feelings, we may have a lot of them to feel. We may have been denying them for a long time, so we may at times feel almost overpowered with rage. We needn't be alarmed; we can deal with each issue one at a time. If serious issues from childhood begin to force themselves out, a trained counselor is definitely needed.

This topic is something that I learned a great deal about from life experience. I have said that my life took an unexpected, dramatic change some years ago. I was totally unprepared for the events that unfolded. And anger was the overriding emotion that I felt. And yet, I felt guilty for being angry because I could see that the situation was not one of anyone's choosing. Still my life was being disrupted big time and I was angry. It was so unfair. Now I felt trapped, trapped between anger and guilt, not a good place to be. I was angry; I knew I was angry, but I felt ashamed of being angry when others were suffering more than I was. And at that time some well-meaning friends reacted as the person I described above, when I had been dealing with a much smaller incident; they told me that it was no one's fault. How could I be angry? After all, thank goodness that such and such had not happened.

Being the recipient of such talk taught me in the clearest way possible how very unhelpful it is for people to try to talk us out of our feelings. I only felt worse. With help I learned to deal with my angry feelings, to appropriately express them and then to begin to move on with my life. The next chapter on crisis will explore this topic in more depth.

Monitoring our feelings with regard to anger is a very necessary part of making our lives work. We cannot get on with fully developing our talents, our skills, using only a portion of our minds. When we allow anger to occupy any part of our minds for a long period of time, we slow and perhaps stop our creative flow. And we may cause damage to our physical bodies as well. Being angry is appropriate at times, but it must be dealt with in a manner that is also appropriate.

Crisis

Let its lessons free us.

✛ ✛ ✛

Chapter Six

✠ ✠ ✠

Crisis

When our lives work, we pause without judgment when crisis hits; and we allow ourselves recovery time, knowing that we are worth that effort.

What is a crisis anyway? The dictionary defines it as a turning point, a crucial time. I found that interesting since that was certainly not how I would have thought of any crisis in my life. I thought of it as a time of disaster, a time of my being out of control. Until recently I would not have said that a crisis was a turning point. It felt like a time that I was stuck, unable to get on with my life. But I do speak from experience when I say it is possible to come through things that you never thought you could ever get through. And not only is it possible to come through, it is possible to come through stronger. It turns out that a crisis can be a gift that gives our lives a new and better focus. It's not a gift most of us welcome with open arms, but when the events in our lives seem to be overwhelming, it can be helpful to think of this definition of a crisis: a turning point. We can change direction, and change for the better. Like the mythological phoenix bird, we can rise again from what may seem like the ashes of our life.

But in order to do that, we have to know some things about

crisis, about coping with what we may label as disasters. Often two things stop us from dealing effectively with the trauma that hits our lives:

1. We pretend to ourselves that it really isn't so bad.

or

2. Although we understand it is bad, we don't allow ourselves any time to recover.

Why would we try to convince ourselves that something which was upsetting to us was really not that worrisome? The answer, I think, is that many of us have been conditioned to only allow certain events to be considered crises, just as we have allowed ourselves to be angry only over certain circumstances. Bereavement and serious illness and divorce are probably acceptable to be termed crisis. (Even in those cases we tend to lose sight of how widespread the feeling of crisis goes. A divorce, for example, is not just a crisis for the couple and their children, but also for their parents, perhaps their brothers and sisters, and close friends as well.)

But the actual definition of a crisis is anything that makes us feel a sense of loss — *Anything* which makes *us* feel a sense of loss. That is to say, for someone else it might not be such a big deal. That is not the point. If it is a big deal to us, we have to acknowledge that fact and follow the steps required to get ourselves through the difficult period.

Since anything that engenders a feeling of loss is a crisis, such things as moving house, getting older, having to modify a diet for health reasons, or maybe even selling a car or giving away a comfortable piece of furniture that held special memories can all, for a time, make us feel unsettled and uneasy.

Exercise: Bearing in mind the definition of crisis, list any crises in your own life in the past year.

Now answer these questions: Did you discover that you

had experienced more difficult times than you had allowed yourself to acknowledge? And did you allow yourself time to work through each of those painful episodes?

What many people find is that much has happened to them that has been upsetting, many more things than they had thought. Usually this is because we often censure our grief. We don't allow ourselves to believe that we can't handle something that we think other people have handled just fine. So we try to tell ourselves that we really are not upset. But it is impossible to be enthusiastic when we are kidding ourselves about how we really feel; it is so important to allow our true feelings to come to the surface so that we can deal with them It does us absolutely no good to pretend we don't feel what we really are feeling.

Sadly, it is true that if we are feeling bad about something which seems small in comparison to the big tragedies of life, we often don't want to let anyone, least of all ourselves, notice that we are upset about such a "trivial matter." So we pretend we aren't bothered. It is always interesting to watch the body language of people as they speak – it never lies. Every day there exists the potential for us to feel a loss of something, perhaps even the retirement of a clerk in a store where we always shop. Now this doesn't mean that we will be spending all of our days wallowing in loss of every little thing. Sometimes all it takes is a sentence or two so that we acknowledge how we are feeling. "I'm sorry that I won't be seeing her in this store anymore," or "I will miss this place where I have had so many good times" can be enough.

At times, for all of us, life hurts.

It may be a little hurt; perhaps a friend or family member doesn't remember our birthday. We pretend that we aren't really upset. After all, we know they still care, but somehow we

83

feel rejected. There is nothing wrong with us if we feel that way; we are not weak people because we have feelings and sometimes they get hurt. The important thing, however, is to accept that this is the situation. Because hurt and being angry are closely related, the advice given for dealing with anger works here. Even though it may seem a small crisis, we still need to deal with it. We need to talk it out with someone or write about it, perhaps cry about it, whatever we need to do until when we think of that event, we feel calm. Often it can help to try to understand *why* the other person has hurt us. And it may help to look at what our expectations are, how we think people "should" behave. Perhaps we need to review our thinking pattern in that regard. We'll look at both of these issues in the next chapter on forgiveness.

But if instead of doing any of these things, we try to sweep our feelings under the carpet of our consciousness, somewhere down the road these emotions will make themselves known; usually the way they make themselves known either hurts us or hurts another. And, in addition, we never resolve the issue. The pain stays with us; the enthusiastic life eludes us. We may be able to forget it for a time, especially if we stay really busy, but we are denying ourselves the chance to feel real peace. Peace comes when we have worked through our negative feelings. It comes when we have looked at them and then done whatever works for us to release them.

When an "acceptable" tragedy strikes, one that we feel safe in acknowledging, we do perhaps own up to our feelings of grief, but still we often allow ourselves very little time to regroup, to regain our sense of well-being. Unfortunately, today's world doesn't help us at all. Even when people experience a major crisis, it seems their friends and family allow them only a brief time to adjust, to take care of necessary arrangements, and then they expect that the person will be back to "his old self" within a couple weeks. And we praise people who seem to be coping so well in such a short time, making it that much harder for them to allow their true feelings of pain to be recognized.

The experience of a friend of mine whose mother died is typical. Sarah's company was most considerate and understanding when she called to let them know of the death. They told her to take as much time as she needed. They sent lovely flowers on the day of the funeral. Several individuals stopped by at her home or called on the phone. But when, two weeks later, Sarah returned to work, she was expected to be "back to normal." Oh yes, the first day everyone asked how she was doing and said they were glad to see her back, but on day two she was expected to be meeting all obligations as she had done before. Her grieving should now be over, or at least it should not be impacting on her work day.

The result of this attitude, both on the part of her coworkers, and then on Sarah herself, was that she tried hard to keep up with everything. For a time she was able to do so, but within six weeks she was in bed with a serious flu-type illness. She missed nearly a month of work. Probably that time off would have been unnecessary if Sarah had been able to take the time she needed at the time of her mother's death. It is true, of course, that people cannot take unlimited time off from work, but it is also true that a little understanding of what Sarah was feeling would have paid big benefits. She might have been slower in getting back up to speed in her work, but instead she was off work for a total of six weeks. So who benefited in the long run? No one.

When confronted with crisis, remember:

1. We need to look first to our own needs when we are faced with a crisis.

As we have said over and over, we can not be any good for

anyone else until we are good for ourselves. This means we have to take care of ourselves when crisis hits. We have to allow ourselves to feel the pain, even if we think other people might not be as upset as we are over this particular situation. If something is a crisis for us, it is a crisis. That's all there is to it. And if it is a crisis, that means we have to deal with it.

If other people are also involved in this crisis, as in the cases of divorce and bereavement, it is important for us to recognize their need for help as well. However, *we are in no shape to be their major help resource.* That is very important to realize. In my own life I saw how not acknowledging that fact led to much slower healing in the life of a family member. While I was managing to cope myself, with difficulty, I thought I was also providing the necessary support needed for the others affected by the crisis. I was not. The other people involved needed more support than a grieving person can give. The best thing for a person in this position to do is to seek out qualified people to help each member of the group who is affected.

2. We have to give ourselves the time it takes us to follow the healing steps, realizing that it will take as long as it takes.

No one else can predict for us how long that will be. *We* must not keep going on, "stiff upper lip," pretending that we are managing perfectly in spite of whatever has happened. There is a heavy price to pay when feelings of pain are ignored. It's been said before. Painful feelings kept under wraps will explode somewhere, either in poor physical health, mental illness, and often today in acts of violence. We are people with feelings, with emotions. We have them for a purpose. We pretend they don't exist to our peril.

Recognizing those two pitfalls, then, here are some tips to help the grieving process along. And that is what we are talking about here – grieving. We have to grieve for what we have lost, whether it is a person, a career, better health, even an idea we once really believed.

To cope with crisis:

1. *Relax your expectations of yourself.*

Don't expect that you will carry on as you always have. This is a very hard thing for us to do these days because all around us we hear people praising those who are "soldiering on" despite the most difficult situations. We need to learn to ignore those voices and listen to our own inner voice. We will know inside ourselves when we are ready to move on in our grief process. We can not be all things to all people when we are in pain.

2. *Allow yourself to feel all the feelings.*

Negative feelings are just as valid as positive ones, but they need to be expressed in a *safe* and *healthy* way. Again, we so often make judgments about what we are feeling. We decide we should not have a particular feeling, especially anger, and so we try to pretend we aren't feeling it. This is treading on dangerous ground. Sooner or later that emotion is going to find its outlet, and with much more force than it would have done if expressed early. Remember again that feelings are not right or wrong. They are just feelings. Don't listen to anyone who might tell you that you "shouldn't" feel a particular way. If you feel that way, you do, and you are allowed. How you express that feeling is the only issue.

3. *Talk about your feelings with a trusted person.*

This point cannot be stressed too often. Negative emotions have to be released. Find a person, a trained counselor or friend, who will let you feel safe, safe in your disclosures. It is important to know that whatever you say, you will not damage the relationship, and your words will remain confidential. (For certain issues only a trained counselor will do. Never be afraid to seek this type of help. It is a sign not of weakness, but of strength.)

87

4. Take care of your physical body.

Of course, you won't feel like caring for yourself properly. It is very difficult to take the time to eat anything, never mind food that would be good for you. And sleep is elusive at times for all of us, and a crisis makes it only more so. Still it is critical that we *try* to follow all the healthy habits that we can. Everything is worse when we don't feel well physically. Our body is having enough to cope with as we try to come to terms with whatever crisis has hit us. We need to help it keep from becoming too run down. This is a good place to enlist the help of friends. Ask them to assist in providing food or offering to go for walks or whatever. People are generally very willing to help when they know of a need.

5. Eventually, do something that you feel good about doing – for yourself and to help others.

The key word here is *eventually*. Don't try too soon to get back in the swing of things. Take small steps in your path of recovery. In so many arenas the world is a better place because of those people who took their time to grieve; then they had the resources to put some good back into the world. Like those who overcome their anger, the people who have finished their grieving have begun support groups, written books, campaigned for more safety on our roads, in our homes, and at places of employment. They have become valuable as safe, non-judgmental listeners. But none of them would have been able to do these things if they had not first considered their own needs and given themselves the time and the space they required.

Those people who grieve for their losses for as long as it takes come through as stronger people. And those people also tend to find their worlds a much better place than they had previously thought. A crisis, far from being a totally terrible event, has the power to make us stronger, more peaceful people.

It truly is a turning point that can enrich our lives. But to get to that point, we have to do our grieving work.

How can friends help a person in crisis?

This chapter, while basically written for the person dealing with crisis, can also offer some suggestions for those of us who may come in contact with grieving friends or family members. While there are many groups who offer support for particular tragedies, some of us will not have the necessary time for their training and yet would like to know what to do when we are confronted with people in pain.

1. Never *tell any person that he should not be feeling any particular way.*

In fact, if a person says, "I shouldn't feel this way," assure them that it is perfectly all right to feel that way now. As people have time to talk out how they feel, the vehemence with which they feel something begins to subside. I have seen how it happens in my own life. When I have been in the midst of some of the most difficult times, I am so grateful to have found caring, non-judgmental listeners. I can recall many conversations in which I heard myself saying things like, "I just don't see how I can cope with this any longer. I don't see any way out." Sounds pretty desperate to me now, even as I write these words. And yet, as the conversation continued, with my listener merely responding with words like, "Yes, I can see why you feel that way," instead of with words like, "You shouldn't feel that way," I made my own way out of my pain. I was able to continue on.

2. *Make time for a grieving person.*

Some of us need to look at our priorities in life. Too many of us are so busy with things that are not really that important that we don't have time to be interrupted, to have our schedule changed. A friend once told me of an incident she experienced. She had called someone in an emergency to ask if she could drive a person in great need to a hospital. The person she called replied that she would like to but she was on her way to a meeting. She was not leading this meeting; she was just attending. Do we have our priorities right?. People in pain do not necessarily appear at convenient times. When we genuinely cannot stop, it is important to suggest a lifeline, perhaps another person. Or we can offer to be contacted later, and then we must make sure that we really are available then. Again it is important to consider what the big picture of life is. Contrary to what appears to be the case by the way we often run our lives, people do matter more than material possessions. How many times do we hear children saying they wish they could spend more time with their parents? And it is just not children who feel lonely in today's world. More and more people find themselves alone too much. While some of the responsibility must lie with them – there are all sorts of volunteer activities around – still, we need to examine our own lives to see if we could make some changes so that we would have more time available to support others.

3. Never indicate by words or actions that we think anyone is taking a long time to get over his or her particular grief.

As has been said, it takes as long as it takes, and nothing slows the process more than an impatience for it to be finished. This does not mean that we help people to stay stuck. We can suggest small steps that they may want to try. We can help build their sense of their own strength by reminding them of the progress they are making, even if that progress seems slow to us. But implying in any way that they are taking too long only further injures an already hurting person.

4. Allow people to cry in front of us.

For some of us, tears are a threat to our own sense of control. Because this is so, we are afraid to let others cry when they need to do just that. Crying is good for us; it releases our emotions and alleviates the pain. If we find that we cannot deal with another person's show of pain, it may be important for us to look at why that is so. Are we actually afraid of allowing some pains of our own to surface? When a person finds himself in the position of crying a great deal of the time, however, it is usually important that a trained person be called in. This is generally a sign that there is much to work through, perhaps a great deal of grief kept over a period of years. This can be more than an untrained friend can handle.

5. Help people to recover, to help themselves.

Do not create dependency. This is often the tendency, as we mentioned in the chapter on control. It is easy to take on too many of the responsibilities of the grieving person, not helping them, but really taking over. This does not help anyone to get stronger; it may seem to aid in the grieving process temporarily but in the long run it does not help develop a strong, independent person. Helping a grieving widow or widower to do some of the jobs that the spouse used to do, for example, can be good at first. But taking on and doing those things for the surviving person on a regular basis is not. All of us need help in the beginning of our crisis, but the goal is for us to regain our ability to cope with our own changed lives, not to learn to have to depend on other people.

When we seek to help people in a time of crisis, let us allow them to grieve as they need to grieve. Let us encourage them, but not always do for them. Eventually most of us are able to develop our lives again, changed as they may be. But we need the right kind of help to do this. When the grieving process works, people not only learn to overcome the intense sadness, but they also develop strengths they probably didn't know they had. As we come through the tough spots in life, when we feel the weakest and most vulnerable, we gain confidence in our ability to cope. We also gain a heightened awareness of the good things in life, a heightened ability to be enthusiastic and joyful. Psalm 30:5 says it well: Tears may flow in the night, but joy comes in the morning.

Forgiveness

This is the way to inner peace

✠ ✠ ✠

Chapter Seven

✠ ✠ ✠

Forgiveness

When our lives work, we realize that our ability to forgive others is hampered if we cannot forgive ourselves.

Now we come to a topic that is often very misunderstood. Many people feel that to forgive another is a sign of weakness, a sign that we've allowed another person to "win." Nothing could be further from the truth. People who are genuinely, not superficially, able to forgive are the most courageous of all and the biggest winners. But like much of what we've already talked about, it is not an easy thing to do, to forgive.

Some of us are not even interested in forgiving; we feel that what was done or said to us is so bad that we are entirely justified in remaining angry. Perhaps, but the person who is angry and resentful is the person who is suffering. Don't we owe it to ourselves to move on? For awhile it is natural to tell ourselves that it is someone else's fault that we are upset. But the truth of the matter is that we are responsible for our feelings, not anyone else. We can always choose how we will feel. We can choose negative or positive feelings; it is up to us.

Forgiveness can come only after we have dealt with our anger, not before. That is an important thing to remember. Those of us who believe in the importance of forgiveness sometimes forget that we first have to get rid of the negative feelings we have before true forgiveness can occur. When we try to forgive too soon, when we are not really over our anger, our words may speak forgiveness, but our inner feelings do not. And, as we have said, our bodies keep track of all our negative feelings, as well as of all our good ones.

Exercise: Bring to mind right now a person who is causing you to feel angry, resentful, unhappy in any way. Then ask yourself these questions:

    What exactly is the person doing which is upsetting to me?

    What did he/she do in the past that is still bothering me?

    What might be the reason that person is doing (or did) it?

    Does he/she know that I am upset?

    Are my expectations realistic about how the person should behave?

    What would happen if right now I chose to see the situation differently?

When we look carefully at these questions, it may help us to move forward in the forgiveness process. When we take the time to analyze the situation, we may find that our expectations regarding this relationship are unrealistic. Perhaps we are expecting more from a person than he or she can give at this time. Perhaps we recognize that we are too sensitive, too easily hurt. It may help us to spend some time thinking about why that is the case. Maybe you feel that this person is just "out to get you," that this person has no consideration for your feelings, that he is totally looking out for himself. Can you change your attitude? This may not be easy. We may have tended to think that people are just deliberately choosing to cause us pain, that we are never lucky in our relationships. Another couple of exercises may help us to think differently.

96

Exercise: List the people in your life who have caused you pain.

Exercise: List the people that you have hurt.

Doing that exercise myself always reminds me that I am not blameless myself. Yes, other people may have hurt me more — at least I think so — but every human being has at some time hurt another person. Perhaps that gives a little perspective. The Golden Rule would remind us that we would want to be forgiven. Can we not do likewise?.

Sometimes we are hurt in ways that are so deep that answering those questions will not help. The malicious act of another, sometimes a person even unknown to us, which causes us great bodily harm, or which causes great harm to one of our family members, cannot be forgiven without a great deal of work. But it is still important to begin the forgiving process if we wish to recapture a life with any peacefulness in it. It may help to look at why people do things to us that hurt.

Why do people do things that cause us pain?

1. They think that they are doing whatever they are doing for our own good.

People who criticize whatever we have done think that their critical remarks will help us to improve. People who deny us something so that we will learn whatever lesson they think we need to learn believe that this is helpful. This is about control, as we have seen in chapter four, but few people see what they are doing as that. They see it as caring for us.

A young man was once persuaded, with great difficulty, to do a reading for a church service. He was frightened and didn't really want to do it, but his Sunday School teacher encouraged him. The day came, and with fear and trepidation, he read the passage. It went well for a first-time effort. What happened, however? Two "well-meaning" members of the congregation came up to him afterward and said, "Too bad you didn't speak up. We couldn't hear you." The result was that that young man never returned that church, and I bet it was a long time before he ever stood up to speak in public.

Those two people thought they were helping him. They were not. Yes, it would be helpful if he spoke louder another time, but there was no reason why just then they had to make that comment. (We wonder why we suffer from low self-esteem!) Instead they could have praised his courage and willingness to stand up at all. Another time, if he was scheduled to speak again, someone *tactfully* could mention how important it is to speak loud enough for the people in the back rows to hear.

2. *The second reason people may cause us hurt is very straightforward: they are thoughtless.*

Sometimes we all just forget things. We are so preoccupied, so busy, with our own concerns that we neglect to do what others might expect of us. We don't intend to cause bad feelings; we just are not "fully present," so to speak. If we at times forget other people, and we know that we do, then it follows that they do the same. How many times have we forgotten to send cards for special days or forgotten an important event that was taking place in a close friend's life? We are not perfect, and we should not expect perfection in others. In so many situations the people who let us down didn't have any intention of deliberately hurting us. They were just thoughtless. When we feel that a person is causing us pain, then it is helpful to look more carefully at the situation.

3. *The third reason we may feel that people are causing us pain is that we have unrealistic expectations about what they should be doing.*

Often it isn't they who are causing us the hurt. It is we ourselves. We have decided what we want from them, and when

98

they do not give it, we may become angry and full of resentment.

How many times I have heard people saying, "I just can't forgive the fact that he never gets me a birthday card." Or, "I just can't forgive him for choosing to spend Christmas away from the rest of the family." If we believe that certain things must happen, then, of course, we will be upset when they do not. Perhaps it is important to look at those expectations. If our relationship is good with another person, should it matter if that person always remembers each important event or always conforms to our way of thinking? If we didn't have those thoughts, the need to forgive would not even be a consideration.

Sadly, for too long in my life I have been tripped up by just such thoughts. I was so busy seeing what people forgot to do in regard to me that I never saw what they were doing. I could easily remember the slight I experienced, and just as easily forget the special times the same person had done a kind thing for me. The person who forgot my birthday one year sent me a gorgeous "Thinking of You" card just when I needed most to receive it. Was I grateful? Yes, to a degree, but I still chose to remember how she forgot my birthday. Today I am better. Today I know that I am not perfect myself. I forget things; I have neglected people. Today I am just grateful for all the good that does come my way.

But, our expectations aside, it is true that all of us at sometime or other in our lives will be hurt by someone. We may be physically hurt; members of our families may be hurt which hurts us; we may be hurt emotionally by the actions of others. It doesn't do any good to say they shouldn't have done it. Probably they shouldn't have, but our saying so will not heal us. And healing us is what it is all about. Our lives can't work for us when we keep thinking about how something should not have happened. Maybe it should not have happened, but the truth is, it did. Now what?

99

4. The last reason people hurt us is that they are in so much pain themselves that their pain just spills out everywhere.

And we may happen to be standing in their path. This is a hard concept to take on because if someone is really hurting us, or has seriously hurt us, we don't care why; we just want the pain to stop. But if we can pretend that this situation is happening to someone else, if we can get some perspective, we might see that indeed the children, spouses, neighbors, bosses, whoever, are themselves suffering in some way. People who are suffering are not thinking about our problems, only theirs. They are themselves just trying to get by, and they are either unaware of the pain they are causing, or aware but still unable to stop.

Many people cannot come to grips with this idea. They want revenge; they want punishment; they want the person hurting them to pay. It is very understandable that this will be the first reaction. We are, after all, human. Listening to a talk show recently I heard people who had been wronged, sometimes in very serious ways, speak about how they wanted the person who had hurt them to suffer. They seemed totally unable to see that the person causing the pain was also in pain.

Happy people do not go around hurting other people. Think about a typical day in the lives of all of us. If, while we are away from the house, our day goes well, when we come home we usually have much more patience with anyone who lives with us. But, just let us have had a bad day, one in which several things may have gone wrong. What is our attitude then to those who are unlucky enough to be in the house when we come home? Chances are our conversations with them are not what one would call pleasant and courteous.

This reason, that people who are treating us badly are themselves hurting, is perhaps the most important reason to consider when we are trying to forgive truly serious, nearly unforgivable events. It is also the one reason to remember if circumstances require that we have frequent contact with a person who seems to continually do things that are very hurtful to us. The more pain a person is feeling, the more pain that person will cause. It is people in pain who are responsible for some of the most monstrous acts in our society. This does not mean that they should suffer no consequences for their behavior. It does mean, however, that we should try not to let the actions of their pain destroy our lives. In order for us to accomplish that, we need to understand that no person who is doing well within himself will willfully set out to hurt another. While we will never be able to say that what was done was acceptable, we can begin to free ourselves to begin to regain our lives by recognizing that we or our family members were not the special targets. We just happened to be in the way of a person in extreme pain who had to let that pain out. And, sadly, we are witnessing more and more of these extreme cases of people's pain erupting. Unfortunately, one of the saddest memories of 1999 will be the number of young people who chose to exhibit their pain by shooting their classmates.

How can I stop my pain?

Forgiveness requires action. We cannot just casually say that we forgive someone and really feel the peace that comes from genuinely forgiving. There are five steps to follow:

1. Without emotion — much easier said than done — look at exactly what the other person is doing or has done that makes you hurt.

Perhaps pretend that a good friend has come to you with your problem; now, what advice would you give?

Too often we don't really get to the heart of the problem. Why exactly are we upset? When a relationship is breaking up, what is the real reason for our unhappiness? Is it because we still care for the person, or could it be that mostly we fear being on our own? Is it because we hate for other people to know that this is happening to us? Maybe it is a bit of each of those.

When we look at the different elements of our pain, we can begin to come up with ways to cope with each of them, thereby making forgiveness easier. If fear of being on our own is an issue, we can work on ways to deal with that; if not wanting others to know is the problem, we can begin by telling at least one safe person. If we still care about the person, perhaps we can work on trying to find an amicable way to separate. Whatever we do, when we do something, we feel at least a bit in control of the situation. And when we feel we have some control, we become less angry. Forgiveness becomes more possible.

Please note: Physical and sexual abuse must never be tolerated, and help must be sought to get out of that situation. This book is not meant to deal with ongoing cases of physical or sexual abuse. Forgiveness should never be attempted as a means to stop abuse. It can only be attempted once the abuse has stopped. And forgiveness does not necessarily mean having a relationship with the person who has caused the pain. It just means we eventually can learn to still feel peaceful in ourselves, despite what has happened to us.

2. *After we examine closely what is the real cause of our pain, then we need to look at how we are helping others hurt us.*

Yes, this is something that some situations demand we look at. We are in this too; it's back to that expectations problem. If your adult child living in another city doesn't write to you, and this hurts, why do you have the expectation that caring is shown by letters written? If your spouse never remembers special days, why do you have the expectation that caring is shown by remembering special days?

It is true, sadly, that we miss seeing how people care about us because we fail to understand their way of showing that caring. Consider the wife who feels unloved because her husband never remembers their wedding anniversary, and yet each morning he brings coffee to her in bed, knowing that she is not a morning person and likes to ease into the day. Examples like this abound, of people doing kind things for us that we fail to give them credit for because our expectation is for something different. That is exactly what I was doing when I felt hurt by my friend's forgetting my birthday while she remembered me with a special card at another time.

3. Here comes that familiar advice again: we need to talk about what is bothering us to someone not involved in the situation.

We may need to find a safe way to vent any anger that we feel. Often our reluctance to talk about our pain is caused by our need to seem to be on top of everything, to have it all together. We don't want others to know that we have a problem. If a person has done something to us that others will learn about, we feel doubly vulnerable. This is particularly true in cases of relationship breakups. It is also true when children do unacceptable things that cause public comment.

And so, a part of our anger at the other person may be anger that now the world will know that our life is not achieving the expectations of a "good life." Often the person we need to forgive the most is ourselves. We need to allow ourselves to not always handle everything perfectly. And we have to allow ourselves to let the world know that. It's ok; no one else is handling everything perfectly, either.

4. We need to learn to communicate in a non-hostile way with the person who is causing us the pain.

The person who is hurting us needs to be told this, but told in a gentle, non-accusatory way. How to do this is the subject of the last chapter, but do it we must because then we can help

103

to clarify expectations so that both sides know what they are.

The most unhelpful phrase I hear in my workshops is "Well, if he really cared, he would know that this is upsetting." This is not true! Usually he genuinely doesn't know. And if you are quite certain that he does know, then it is time to look at his pain. Why does he feel it necessary to cause pain? We have said it over and over, but the answer is the same. The mouth speaks what the heart is full of (Matthew 12:34). People in pain cause pain. People who forgive change their worlds.

5. *In matters that are so serious, that involve perhaps the taking of another's life, the best advice for most people is to care enough for themselves to get help from qualified therapists.*

Some things that we need to forgive are just too much for us to handle on our own, even with trusted friends to help us.

Remember you are human, not perfect.

We need, for our own mental and physical health, to learn to forgive others, but an even harder thing to do is to forgive ourselves. We have not done things perfectly up to now, and we will never do things perfectly. Those are the facts. Once we understand that, we can learn to forgive ourselves; we can learn from the errors we make, but then we can go on.

When I finally realized that I didn't have to be perfect, my whole world began to change. When I realized that I would never do everything right, that I would make errors in judgment, that I would forget things, that I would say things I wish I hadn't said, I became more human. And as I became more human, I allowed other people to become more human as well. I am less hard on myself, and the result is I am also not so hard on other people. I am more easily able to take people as I find them. Of course, like all things, I am not perfect at thinking like this all the time either, but I am learning. I have lots less to forgive these days because I don't have such expectations of what others should be doing.

You may be afraid to look into yourself, afraid of what you will see. Some of us have caused a great deal of pain to others, through our own pain. We need to forgive ourselves for that, but perhaps we also need to try to make up for some of what we have done.

Harold Kushner, in his book *Who Needs God,* suggests that a good way to help forgive ourselves is to try to put some good back into the world for whatever we regret doing. This seems to be good advice. Having learned whatever we learned from our divorce, our problems with our children, our loss of employment, we can find a way to help others. We can do volunteer work; we can give money to support causes; we can be open and tell others our experiences, thereby freeing them to talk about their problems; perhaps together we will find solutions.

In order to make our lives work, we must learn to forgive.

When the Bible tells us that we are to forgive one another (Matthew 18:21–35), it is not giving us that advice just so that we will treat others better, though that is part of the reason. But, equally as important is the fact that forgiving others frees us. Sometimes although we forgive, we may not necessarily still retain a relationship. In certain situations it will not be in our best interests to continue to see the persons who have hurt us. Retaining a relationship is not always the goal. And in cases of traumatic loss, grieving will be a large part of the forgiveness process. Forgiving is not easy, but being able to reach a state of forgiveness will bring with it a new sense of peace. When we have that, we can then get on with our lives.

Goals

*Knowing where we are going lets us
know when we have gotten there.*

✠ ✠ ✠

Chapter Eight

✠ ✠ ✠

Goals

*When our lives work, we use our talents for our own
pleasure, and for the good of the community.*

It may seem to some readers that it has taken a long time to
get to what might be considered the real heart of this book:
doing something so that our lives can get better. There is a
reason for this. Before we can begin to achieve on the scale that
is possible for us, we have to have straighten out our thought
process. We recall again those words from Proverbs 4:23: Be
careful how you think; your life is shaped by your thoughts.
Your life is shaped by your thoughts. That says a mouthful. How our
lives go is determined by how we think. The way we think
affects us in our relationships with others, as we have seen, in
whether we can get over the crises in our lives, in whether we
can we learn to forgive and then move on. And how we think
also affects how our careers go, whether our careers are ones
that involve making money or ones that involve caring for
other people without financial reimbursement.

Once we get our minds into a more peaceful state, then –
and only then – are we able to discover what we want our goals

to be, what our purpose is. We may not even realize that we need to consider this question – we are so busy as it is. But just because we may appear content, because we have much to do, that doesn't mean we are busy doing things that bring us deep satisfaction. Hopefully, by the time you have gotten to this chapter in the book, you have become more aware of those changes that you may wish to make. Hopefully, by now you have decided you don't want to spend any more days just getting up each day and doing "things," but not feeling personally fulfilled.

As we continue learning to value ourselves, to become less fearful, as we learn to spend less time managing others and more time checking out our own lives, we will begin to find what works for us in all aspects of our lives. Each of us was given special talents and given these gifts for a purpose. Our goal should be to find ways to use them. When we are doing what we like to do, our lives run better. Few things are worse than having to wake up each morning with dread about the day ahead.

It takes time to change old habits.

It takes both time and patience to change habits that we have had for many years. We will not get it right every time. And sometimes we may have periods when it appears that little is happening. We need those quiet, supposedly unproductive times as well. Too many of us feel that we need to have "accomplished something" every day. That is not true. A quiet day spent in nurturing ourselves can pay immense dividends later.

A good indicator of how are lives are going is the feeling we have when we wake in the morning. While it is natural to have days that the thought of getting out of bed is almost more than we can tolerate, if our lives are working for us, those days should be few. That has been the goal of this book, to help people discover for themselves how they can make some changes in life as it is so that it can become more life as they would like it to be. Goals have gotten a bad "rap" in recent days as companies have often used the term to put pressure on employees to perform to a certain standard. That is *not* at all what I mean when I use the word goal. My definition of a goal is simply something that we need to accomplish, either out of necessity, or for our own pleasure. And that goal may be to do nothing the world would call productive for some period of time, to give ourselves some time to step back and assess our situations. And then ideally, as we make our lives work, we adopt a lifestyle that suits us so well that most of our goals become ones that bring us pleasure.

Part of the reason we feel at times that we are not living satisfying lives is that we don't give ourselves credit for all we are doing, all the goals we are meeting. In any given day we accomplish all sorts of things, from getting ourselves to certain destinations, making necessary phone calls, doing chores around the house, fulfilling work requirements, and so on. Yet, when I ask people, "What have you accomplished today?" the answer I generally get is, "Not much."

When I then ask them to list what they have done, the lists are long. In actual fact many goals are accomplished every day, but we don't see that if we think of goals as only big important accomplishments. Some goals are major. Goals may involve changing a job, changing an entire career, moving to a new location, or perhaps taking on a big responsibility for a volunteer organization. But much of the time those are *not* the kind of goals that we encounter. Goals of that magnitude don't happen every day, but each day we do have other things that we do, goals that we want to accomplish.

What's the point of looking at our everyday list of things to do as goals?

There are two reasons:

1. When we actually take the time to look at what we do each day, we see that indeed we are accomplishing much.

It gives us a sense of satisfaction, a sense of well-being to see just how much we do get done in any given day.

2. When we see what we are doing each day, and the time being taken, we can see a pattern developing.

When we look at that pattern, we can decide if that is the way we wish to spend our days, or if it is not.

Our well-being seems to require that we continually strive for something that we do not currently have. But we are not talking about material things here exclusively, though they are a factor at times. If getting "things" becomes the only goal we have, however, life soon loses its meaning. We need to be working toward a result that is currently not in our grasp. We need to be stretching our abilities.

It is vital that our goals reflect our own interests and talents, not someone else's. They need to be geared toward what is suitable for us in any particular stage of our lives. A mother with very small children may not find it practical currently to have as her objective going back to school for further education. A man or woman with family financial responsibilities may not at this time be able to just quit work. But that does not mean that these people might not be keeping that goal in the backs of their minds, and thus they could be on the lookout for opportunities that will eventually help that goal to happen.

Just as validly our goals might be such small ambitions as finding a half hour in a busy day to read a magazine, or taking ourselves out for a cup of coffee to sit and watch the world go by, or spending some time in the public library researching a hobby, or repotting some plants, or any other activity which is not part of our usual everyday life.

It's important that we have goals. And it is important that we take steps to bring them to fruition. Too often we just go through our days, hardly noting what we are doing. We talk of ways that we would like to change our lives, but talk is all we do. Then at some point we may be pulled up short, forced to realize that we have spent much of our time in ways that didn't really suit us at all. There is no point in waiting. It's time now to discover what suits us, and it's time now to begin doing it.

In order to achieve our goals, we will have to take action.

Because you are reading this book, presumably you do want your life to be different, to work better, but making that happen, as we have been saying all along, takes work. It doesn't occur overnight. It takes courage, too, because change can be upsetting at first. It is scary to break out of old molds. You've come this far; you can do it. You can make your life work for you.

Goals do not become realities by just thinking about them. Writing this book taught me that; it should be obvious, but somehow we sometimes miss the obvious. For some time people had been saying to me, "You should write a book." I thought so too, but I thought of all the time it would take, and would it get published, and was it worth all the trouble? As silly as it sounds, I saw myself as the author of a book, but I didn't see myself writing it! I was doing the thinking all right, but I was not taking any action. And the same thing happened again when I began to realize that I needed to revise and update this book. I wanted it done, but I didn't want to do the work it would take to make it happen.

Goals are basically promises we make to ourselves.

Some of these promises we make to ourselves are really for other people. We promise ourselves we will get that report to our boss on time, or we will make those crafts for the bazaar. These promises are easier to keep. The hardest ones to keep are those we make to ourselves *for* ourselves. Almost anything can stop us. Suppose, for example, you are promising yourself a morning in the library by yourself when you get a phone call from a friend who is at loose ends and wants you to take in a museum with her. How many of us have the courage to keep our promise to ourselves and go to the library? How many would drop their own plans and go with the friend, though they really didn't want to? Certainly, some situations demand that plans be changed, but think what we would have done if we had had a dental appointment at that same time. We would have no guilt then about saying that we were not free.

Why are we so reluctant to make and keep promises for ourselves?

1. It may be lack of self-esteem.

Everyone else's plans matter more than ours, we may think. If you think this is the case for you, it may be helpful to reread chapter two. When we don't feel good about ourselves, it is very difficult to say no. We live in such fear of hurting other people's feelings that we find ourselves continually doing things that we don't want to do. Though we may have promised ourselves to spend some time taking an aerobics class, for example, we can easily be swayed to drop that plan if it appears that our doing so would inconvenience someone else. The surest guarantee of failure is trying to please everyone. It can't be done, for one thing, and, secondly, it stops us from having our own lives. Instead we are being controlled by other people's needs too much of the time.

2. It may be that we haven't taken the time to look at what we really like to do, at how we actually would enjoy spending our free time.

It seems that the prescription for the "right" sort of life has been so programmed for us by society's values. It's about the right education, the right career, the right marriage, all at the appropriate ages. In our desire to follow this path we can become so preoccupied with doing it all that we forget to check to see if this path is right for us. It may be right for many, but that does not mean it is right for us. We may be spending so much time doing things to meet those ends that we have no time left to do the things we would rather be doing. And in the process, we may realize one day that we have forgotten what we really do enjoy. Perhaps the next exercise will help to unlock some unexplored areas of your life, ones that you may now wish to pursue.

3. It may be that we find ourselves in a family situation that is extremely difficult.

It may be that dealing with that situation is taking whatever energy we have. It may be that we are in the middle of a crisis. As we said in the previous chapter, sometimes the promises we make to ourselves may have to do with not doing as much as we would normally feel capable of doing. I know that for me there remain periods in my life when family concerns are so overwhelming that my goal for that time is to reduce my obligations and double the time spent nurturing myself so that I can continue to cope. Sometimes it may be hard for us to acknowledge that we can't do it all, but it is important that we allow ourselves time to recover. It is important that we do what is necessary to sustain ourselves. While we may feel frustrated because we are not accomplishing what we wish we were accomplishing, we will have achieved nothing if we eventually find ourselves so ill that we can no longer cope with our daily lives.

But, assuming that you are not in the place of having major emotional struggles at the moment, perhaps this exercise will help you to take steps to make positive changes in your life.

Exercise: Think what you would like to accomplish in each of the following areas of your life, and write your ideas down. Make two lists, one of things you would like to do this year and one for future years.

Area One: *Your relationships with other people.*

Do you want to entertain more, make more time for special friends? Maybe you want to consider limiting the amount of time now being spent with a certain person or group of people. Maybe you need to work on repairing a certain relationship. Perhaps you are interested in meeting some new people.

Area Two: *Your current living accommodation.*

Do you want any changes in location or decoration? Do you have ideas, large or small, of ways to alter a particular room or rooms? It might be that you just would like to find a corner that could become your "quiet" corner. It might involve changing the color scheme. Feng Shui is the study of our environment's impact on our emotional lives. It might be of interest to learn more about this.

Area Three: *Your current career, or purpose in life.*

Does it need rethinking? If you have primarily been a parent, for example, but now the children are getting more independent, what is next for you? Is your job still satisfying, or have you been wishing you could change it? Perhaps a modification in the volunteer activities you now do is indicated. Think about how you feel when you get up in the morning; that is your clue to how you are being affected by your day-to-day activities.

Area Four: *Your leisure time.*

Are you still finding satisfaction in whatever you do in your free time? Maybe it is time to try something new, take a class to learn another skill, perhaps. And if you have too little leisure time, something needs to be done to change that. Either priorities have to change or other people need to help more in the running of things, whether at work or at home. It may be time to consider whether some of what is keeping you busy really needs to be done at all – think again of the big picture of life.

Area Five: *Your physical body.*

Are you getting enough exercise, enough sleep, and eating sensibly? If not, what needs changing? Today there are many alternative care techniques you might want to try to further help your physical body to cope with the stresses you encounter. My shiatsu and reflexology massages are things I make sure to find the time and money to have in my schedule. Taking care of myself so that I have energy is a very important component of a life that works. It is hard to make constructive decisions and changes when we are not feeling well.

Exercise: Taking your list from the above questions, what steps can you take this week to start heading down the path of meeting those goals?

We have seen that goals come in many categories, and each individual has to decide his own. Our lives work once we begin to take more control of our lives, by making promises to ourselves, and then by taking the action required to keep them.

Goals change as our lives change.

Goals are not carved in granite. At times some goals may need to be abandoned, and there is no harm in that. When we leave school, we begin careers with certain goals in mind. Later we may choose, or be forced, to change careers. Our goals will have changed. When we begin families, we have certain goals; if we must face separations from family members, we need to have other goals. If we relocate, we will have different options, thus a chance for different goals.

When business required my husband and me to relocate in England, leaving our family members in the States, goals had to change. The way I used to spend my time had to change. It is not helpful to stay locked into one way of thinking, one set of goals, when circumstances change. That is a sure road to unhappiness. I had to accept that no longer would much of my time be given to family matters. What next then? Developing my own career was the "what next" for me. Others find different answers. The only requirement is that the answer must suit each individual.

I've said it more than once: our lives are a gift. They are meant to give us joy, and out of our joy, we will also find the way to help others. What we give out of pleasure is a true gift. What we give out of resentment is not. That is why it is so important that we begin to make our lives work for us. As we begin to do those things which we find satisfying, we become more enjoyable to be around. We still will feel the negative emotions, like anger and resentment, but less often; we will become too busy getting on with our own lives to spend time getting upset at others.

The biggest reason of all to have goals:

Our earthly lives do not go on forever. Let me repeat, this life does not go on forever. We all know that, of course, but we seem to not want to think about it. We bury our heads in the sand and pretend we have all the time in the world. We think in five years or ten years or whatever, we will then do what we want to do, or have what we want to have. We can't afford to wait. We must begin today to make our lives more workable for us. God gave us life, but it is up to us to live it.

Many people who have been told they have terminal ill-nesses examine their lives for the first time. Some of these people then make some dramatic changes in their lifestyles;

some even overcome their illnesses, or at least greatly extend their lives. It's important to take stock of our lives at periodic intervals and see if they are suiting us. Delaying only postpones our eventual happiness.

Yes, some of our goals we know must be for the future, and we have to hope that we will be able to realize them. But right now, right this minute, we need to begin to work on those things which really matter to us. That is key: *Those things which matter most to us.* This does not mean we forgo our responsibilities, but it does mean we begin to reorganize our lives to find some time to do those things that give our lives meaning.

One woman told me of a conversation she had with a close friend who was dying. Her friend, tears in her eyes, said, "I always felt that I was supposed to do something important, but I just never tried to discover what it was." Well, each of us has the chance right now to try to uncover what it is that is important for us to do. Our goal may not matter to many, but if it matters to us, then it is important.

When we have goals, each morning we have a reason to put our legs out on the floor and get moving. Just remember that some mornings our goals need to be about taking special care of ourselves. In the next chapter we will look at the ways of going from the deciding stage to the action stage. What do you want to accomplish? Now let's look at how to get it.

Getting Started

The first step is the place to begin.

✠ ✠ ✠

Chapter Nine

✠ ✠ ✠

Getting Started

When our lives work, we give ourselves the time to see where we want to go, and then we take steps to begin that journey.

H
ere we come to the hardest part, the beginning. We all know that nothing gets done unless someone does it. We often want the results, but we don't want to take the action. Why not? In the previous chapters we have looked at some reasons.

We have seen that life up to now for some of us has not been conducive to our developing a good image of ourselves. If we don't think well of ourselves because we have lots of guilt, or because the messages we've recieved about ourselves have been negative, it is very hard to get motivated to do things which give us pleasure. If we don't think we have much ability anyway, it is especially hard to motivate ourselves to take action. Instead, we may do many things that we *think* give us pleasure, but in reality they don't actually make us feel good. (Addictions may have become our answer.) Part of us may want to take Italian, let's say, with the goal to eventually travel to Italy. But we don't sign up. Why? We may think we could never learn a foreign language, now, at our age. Or perhaps we think, "I'd never get the money to travel so why set myself up for disappointment?" We might feel that no one in our family has ever traveled overseas, so why should we even consider the idea. Or there might be something in us, frequently deeply hidden, which makes us feel that we don't deserve to have a good life anyway.

Mark was such a person; his early life experiences of an overly strict, critical parent had left him feeling inferior, undeserving. When ideas of things he wanted to do would come into his mind, he immediately dismissed them. He felt that for him life was just something to be endured, not enjoyed. It took time on his own, doing some of the exercises in this book, as well as time spent with new friends, friends who were much more supportive. But eventually he began to understand that just because an adult had said certain things about him, that did not make them right. Little by little, he began to realize that he did have value. Then he was able to get started on his own journey; he started by joining a beginners' class in watercolor painting. Today he understands that he may never set the world on fire with his painting, but the pleasure and relaxation it gives him are well worth the time he spends. And his friends feel lucky to receive some of his work as gifts.

Negative, emotional thought patterns can stop us from getting on with our lives – it can't be said too often. Some of us are so fearful that we refuse to try anything new. We are so afraid of what other people will say, and we are particularly afraid of what will happen if we fail. We forget that failure is just a means to learn something new. Actually, our best lessons come from failure.

Ted came from a family to whom winning was everything. Competition was the focus. The family members competed in all phases of their lives. Discussion was always about who had, or who was, the best. Ted felt uncomfortable with this way of life, especially as he saw the attitude the family members had about those they identified as failures.

As a result, Ted became extremely quiet, but inside himself war was raging. He wanted to try a new career, but he knew it was not one his family would find acceptable. It was not especially lucrative, nor would it be considered prestigious. Fear of being a failure in the eyes of his family kept stopping him. After several months of learning to listen to his own inner voice, he eventually began to update his résumé. He's begun going on interviews. As this book went to press, he has not yet gotten a new job, but as he says, "Life seems so much better," because he has begun his own journey.

Allowing our anger and our need to control others to take over our lives also stops us from taking the necessary actions to make our lives work. Few of us can honestly say that we, at times, do not try to control other people. If we are parents or are in a serious relationship, we undoubtedly have times when we want someone to act in a certain way; and we may spend a great deal of time and effort trying to get them to do so. We often get angry when they refuse. All that time we spend focusing on someone else's actions is time we could instead be using to our own benefit.

Besides benefiting us, it would be positive for the relationship. Letting people have their own lives pays big rewards in peaceful, harmonious living. When I learned to stop trying to manage everyone else, I found the time to more effectively manage me. And I got on much better with those around me as well.

Only as we become more at peace with ourselves will our lives begin to take off in the ways that we want them to go. Only now will practical tips work; no method works for the person who is not fully present to take it in. And *we are not fully present when we are worried, angry, in crisis, or thinking poorly of ourselves.* When we fix our insides, our outside life takes dramatic turns for the better.

When we see that it is we who have to make things happen, when we see that to blame others or the situation is just an excuse, then at last we can begin to make the changes that we want to make. We've looked at many reasons why we find it hard to *act*. Assuming that we are working on all the other reasons why it may be hard to start, now let us look at some time-honored ways to actually get our own particular ball rolling. These suggestions will get us started. Perhaps we may first of all need to change how we do things, perhaps become more efficient.

And now we begin:

Tip One: Remember that the purpose of becoming more efficient is to have more time to do what we really want to do.

Lack of time is the number one reason people give for not doing what they really want to do. (Lack of money is second.) Often the reason we don't have enough time is that we take too long doing the things we don't like to do. We may do this because we dislike doing them so much that, lacking any enthusiasm, we just naturally take longer. We don't see quicker ways of doing the same job. Or, if we don't take longer at the immediate job, we take a long time actually settling down to do it. We put it off, often by doing really non-essential things, just so we don't have to do that despised job.

When we dread getting down to a job, however, that must be done, we become experts at coming up with all sorts of delaying tactics. We may suddenly decide that we must read a magazine article right now; we may decide a cup of coffee is crucial immediately; we may decide we have to phone someone this minute; or we may have to watch a sports event. We can be very creative in the ways we avoid doing things!

Balancing the checkbook is just such a job for me. I hate to do it; the result is that on the day I finally decide I will do it, I put it off and put it off. I water plants that probably don't even need to be watered; I call people I don't really need to speak to;

126

I take an exceptionally long time reading the paper, all just to put off doing what needs to be done. I waste time doing what I don't particularly want to do either, just to avoid doing what I *really* don't want to do.

We all have the ability to find the time for the things that really matter. But it takes looking at our typical days and weeks and seeing where we are spending time in ways that for us are wasteful, not fulfilling, and not necessary.

Tip two: Look again at your old expectations.

The old expectations of how a home or lawn should look, or how perfectly some chores "should" be done may have to change. In the workplace, as well, we may spend too much time on certain jobs that don't need to be done so perfectly. One good friend of mine admits that other people in her office get the job done in a manner that is satisfactory to management, but she sets such high standards that she often has to work overtime to finish. This overtime work, of course, takes away from time that she could be spending doing those things which she chooses for herself.

We may need to change our expectations of *how* we do certain jobs, and we may need to change our expectations of what jobs *must* be done. It's been stated in previous chapters — we can make choices; we can choose to eliminate some things from our lives in order to find the time for what we really want to do. But it requires knowing what we want to do and having a strong commitment to accomplishing it. There is no better time than now to begin.

Perhaps we are going to need to look at the scheduling of jobs within our family group. Sometimes old expectations of *who* should do what are getting in our way. One family found several changes gave benefits to everyone. When Susan wanted to take an evening class three nights a week, she was pleased to have her husband take over the cooking for those three nights;

she had never encouraged him to take any role in the kitchen before, always thinking it was the wife's place to fix meals. He was pleased to do this in exchange for Susan's taking over many of the chores in the yard, chores she found she enjoyed much more than the "nside" ones and ones which were easier for her to fit into her new schedule.

Or consider the case of George who felt it was his job to do all the paperwork of the marriage, from bills to tax and insurance forms. Then he decided he would like to take flying lessons. His busy life made him extremely reliant on a schedule. The flying lessons were on the night that he had previously set aside to do his paperwork. This situation gave his wife Joan just the opportunity she had been hoping for. She had repeatedly asked to take over this responsibility, but George had always said no, believing it was the man's role to handle the family finances.

Our expectations of how a job should be done and who must do it need constant revising if we are to find the time to do those things which give us real satisfaction. The surprising thing, as the two examples above show us, is often that as we satisfy ourselves, we satisfy others. We all want pleasantness in our lives. As we feel more content, we are more pleasant. Let's not let false expectations stand in our way of finding that sense of contentment.

Tip three: Consider your lifetime goals.

Look back at that list of goals you drew up in the last chapter. Decide which have the greatest priority. Think again about what you want to have done in this life. Now that you have found some free time in your days, what do you want to have accomplished? What do you want to be remembered for? What are you doing now that really matters? So much of what we are doing doesn't matter in the bigger picture.

The one caution here is this: our goals need to be realistic for us. For example, I love to sing, but suffice it to say, my singing voice will win no awards anywhere! For me to decide that I want to sing professionally would be totally unrealistic. For me that would not be a logical goal. Instead, for me to find as many chances to sing along with large groups, (where my vocal ability will do the least harm!) is a reasonable concept.

Some people in their middle years won't set any goals because they feel they have missed their chance to have the goal they really wanted. Maybe it is too late to be a professional golfer, but it isn't too late to take up the sport. Achieving a goal is not about being a success as the world views success. As a coffee mug I use says, "Success is doing what you love." That's all there is.

Tip four: When we know where we are going, we need to do some brainstorming by ourselves and with others.

Brainstorming means at first to consider *every* path to your goal. It means to write down every way that you can think of to get to where you want to be. Do not judge that you don't have enough money, or time, or equipment or whatever yet. Just write down everything. Take some time to do this. Then, and only then, begin to take stock of which ones might work, perhaps with some adaptation.

Ask your friends for help. Again this can be a big stumbling block — we hate to act like we need help. We want to be seen to be totally self-sufficient. And yet, why are people here, if not to help each other? What is life all about, if not about people? All the money, all the innovations are useless without a market. Businesses have faltered because management did not take enough time to discover what people really wanted; instead they went ahead with their own ideas, totally disregarding potential consumers.

We have to consider that as well, whether our goals involve selling something to the public or not. Whatever we do, we always impact on other people, whether family members, friends, customers, or co-workers. It only makes good sense to ask those who will be affected for some input about our ideas. (Chapter ten will discuss *how* we present our plans.)

Exercise: On paper identify clearly your goal. The key word here is clearly. Some of us make such general statements that we have no hope of getting to the goal. If your goal is a trip, for example, define exactly where, for how long, and so forth. It is insufficient to just say, "I'd like to travel."

Then:

1. Talk it over with several people, both those who will be immediately and directly affected and any others who will be less involved.
2. Come up with several possible solutions or ways to start.
3. Narrow these down to a few.
4. Allow time out, a time to just let your subconscious deal with the issue.
5. Trust your intuition.

This is key. We need to learn to listen to our own inner voice. Only we actually know what works for us. Other people can have very good insight into our strengths and weaknesses, but it is we alone who really know what we should be doing with our talents. By listening to our own thought patterns, we will find solutions to many things in our lives. Logic and reason alone are not enough. We know ourselves better than we think we do. It is important to listen to what our intuition, our inner voice, tells us.

Tip five: Taking frequent short breaks from our routine gives large rewards.

Studies show that the really efficient person may spend less time actually doing the required tasks; he regularly spends time giving his physical body a break. Instead of sitting at a computer terminal for hour after hour, or at a sewing machine, or at a workshop, the most efficient people schedule periodic breaks.

When we habitually allow time away from our current activity, we give ourselves a much needed respite. In the end we will accomplish much more in a shorter time if we allow our minds a rest by forgetting for a time what we have been doing. This is hard for some people to see. They say they don't have time to take time off. Try it and see. It really works. The mind, like every other part of our body, deserves a rest.

It is tempting to want to rush toward completion, toward our goal. I know. I have to consciously slow myself down, consciously stop what I am doing for a time. I really want to reach my goal ten minutes after I have discovered what it is! But here, also, I am learning. Getting to our goal should be a large part of the pleasure. After all, once we arrive, we will be looking for another goal anyway.

Tip six: Learn how to communicate the changes in your life to the people who will be affected.

One of the reasons that stops us from making needed changes in our lives is our fear of how those around us will react. Whatever we want to change may have some impact on those people that we live or work with, or both. The fear of other people's reaction stops more people than fear of making the change itself. This is true no matter how small the change is. It is true that none of us exists on our own little island. What we decide to do does impact others.

For example, when I decided to become a vegetarian, this was a big change in my eating habits, but it also affected family members and even friends. Now some foods that the family ate, I did not eat. My decision caused some people to then examine their own eating habits; my decision meant meals were different than they had been. Even though meat was still a part of many meals, the fact that one person chooses not to eat it can affect the atmosphere at the table. Also I have several friends that I regularly meet in restaurants for food and conversation. Now we had to begin to look differently at the places that we chose to meet. So, we can see how even a relatively small change that one person makes affects others. It is important to think this through after we have determined the changes we want to make.

It is also important to think through how we will talk about this change. Today, having overcome the health reasons which had caused me to choose the vegetarian diet, I am back to eating some meats. I am grateful for the support I received from friends and family while I was a strict vegetarian. Besides the fact that I have a caring family and caring friends, this particular change worked for me because I did take the time to think about its impact on others and tried to lessen that impact. How we communicate our needs effectively will be the topic of the next chapter. For now, just realizing that making our own changes, whether they involve going back to school, moving, taking a different job, changing the volunteer programs we support, spending more time exercising, changing our eating habits, or anything else also involves our consideration of the way this will change the lives of others.

There you have it, six tips for becoming more efficient, for getting started. I hope they are a beginning for you; I'm confident you will find others that work for you once you are really committed to "going for it." The "it" is yours to choose. Don't miss your chance to develop your skills. We all have them; they are God's gift. Are we using them? Remember that excuses are just things we use when we are not really committed to doing something. Often the biggest reason for excuses is fear. But fear can be conquered. Today we can begin.

Communications Skills

*What we say, when we say it, and how
we say it matter.*

✠ ✠ ✠

Chapter Ten

✛ ✛ ✛

Communication Skills

When our lives work,
we are able to communicate our needs,
at the same time being very aware of the needs of others.

aving spent a great deal of time in this book talking about the importance of looking out for our own needs so that we stay strong enough to be able to help others, it is now time to talk about talking. Proverbs 12:18 reminds us that thoughtless words can wound as deeply as any sword, but wisely spoken words heal. At work and at home and in our neighborhoods how we talk to others can help our lives to work for us. Or, the way we talk to others can cause complications that keep our lives from working as we would like them to work.

So many people forget, in this age of electronics, that ultimately people still matter most. Machines are only as effective as the people running them. The people running them need to feel valued. We've spent time looking at ourselves, trying to see how we can help ourselves to feel better. Now it is time to see how we can help others to feel better also. Too often the words we speak do not have that effect. Too often our language is so critical; too often we forget to praise, but remember easily to find fault. And then we wonder why it is so hard to get along with some people.

We have to have done our work on ourselves first. All our attempts to try to communicate in a caring way will fall on dead ears if we are not sincere in the words we speak. People can always tell. Marge, a woman taking one of my workshops, realized that she had to learn that lesson. On the surface she appeared to converse easily with others; she could be counted on to praise where praise was due. And yet, when she and I talked, she admitted that she really had few friends. People didn't seem to want to get close to her. She had a great many acquaintances, but she didn't feel that anyone really cared about her as a person. She couldn't understand why. She was doing everything right, or was she?

Lots of us have been taught that doing "the right thing" is paramount. The right thing is to help others, to encourage others, and that is certainly true. But people are very clever. We can usually tell when a person really means what he is saying and when he does not. We can tell when people are genuine and when they are not. Maybe we can't tell exactly how we know the difference, but most of us can still recognize insincerity.

At times we may have made mistakes, perhaps trusted someone we should not have trusted. But often, if we were honest, we would realize that we did have an inkling that all was not as it should be. Sometimes we ourselves are so distracted that we do not always see what we would see at other times. But generally, especially over a period of time, we can discover which people we feel safe in calling our true friends.

And that is what had happened to the people who knew Marge. They did appreciate that she was reliable and helpful, I'm sure, but they sensed that she was hiding something. Her manner did not support what her words said. As someone in one of my workshops so aptly put it, "You don't know where you are with someone who is not really being true to herself." Over time Marge came to realize that she actually was very envious of those she was congratulating. When she looked at and recognized her true feelings, she saw that she felt resentful. Her life was not going as she wished, and seeing others who seemed to be succeeding only added to her pain. But, having been taught to do "the right thing," she did what she thought she was the right thing. And it was commendable of her to praise the people that she praised, but it would have worked much better if she possessed the true feelings that went with her words. Now Marge is beginning to look at what her true feelings are, to work out ways to enjoy her own life more. As she does this, as she makes her own life work for her, she will stop sending mixed messages and she will find real friends, not just acquaintances.

It is not just *what* we say, but also very much *how* we say it that matters. While much critical talk is totally unnecessary, it is true that at times we may need to tell people what they do not want to hear. The words we use on these occasions must be chosen with care. That old reliable Golden Rule applies here. Do unto others what you like others to do unto you (Matthew 7:12). We need to think how we would want to be treated if we were the one who needed to be confronted.

When we must offer some input that might be taken as negative criticism, there are two rules to remember:

1. *Always say something positive first.*

2. *Never criticize the person, only the action.*

Suppose you need to tell someone that you cannot recommend him as chairman of the elementary school's fund raising committee. A friend told me of a wonderful way that she heard this situation handled. It seems a person we'll call Jerry was a good friend of Jack's. Jack very much wanted to be chairman of this committee. He had asked Jerry to support him in that nomination, but Jerry felt that for various reasons Jack was not the right person for the job. This can be a difficult situation under any circumstances, when someone asks you to give them support and you don't feel that they are qualified. In this case it was even harder because of the friendship between the two men. But Jerry handled it so well by saying approximately these words: Jack, I know that you are expecting me to support your nomination for chairman of the school's fund raising committee. You have done so much for this school, and I know its continued success really matters to you. However, in thinking about it, I wonder if your demonstrated talent for getting valuable publicity could be better utilized if you were not the chairman. So much of a chairman's job is delegation. Would you instead consider becoming head of publicity?

Perhaps Jack was somewhat disappointed, but he did agree and the men's friendship remained intact. Jerry had reminded him of how good he was at one thing and then asked him to do that. He had given him needed praise, and he had found another valuable job for him to do. Not all situations like this will always work out, of course. But at least we can remind ourselves that we did follow the best possible technique. The results can never be guaranteed, but we will feel better if we know that we acted in good faith and with no intent to harm.

Many times, unfortunately, we refuse to confront a person because we are so afraid of the results. We determine that a person will be upset and so we keep quiet. Usually what happens is that the result is worse than it would have been if we had spoken up in a kind and caring way. It gets worse because generally another situation gets piled on top of the first; then perhaps another until finally one day we just blow up. Our frustration and anger reach such a pitch that confronting someone in a caring way gets totally overlooked. Or we may leave the situation or the person, thereby isolating ourselves when all that would have been needed was a few carefully chosen words.

In our confrontation, however, it is never correct to belittle another person, ever.

How we speak is important. We need to learn to be sensitive to our listener. We may seek to correct a behavior, but we must never define a person as being irresponsible, careless, thoughtless, unreliable, or having any other negative attribute. All of us at some time or another have behaved in just those ways, but that does not mean that that behavior is who we are.

It may be irresponsible, for example, to forget to mail rent money, but that does not mean a person is always irresponsible. It may be thoughtless to forget a wedding anniversary or birthday, but that does not make someone always thoughtless. We are all a mixture of good and bad traits, depending on a given situation.

It is perfectly correct to comment when people let us down, but it is not correct to call them "bad" people because of it. Instead we can say that we are upset because now there is a penalty charge on the rent. And perhaps the person responsible should pay it. Or we can say that we are disappointed that a birthday or anniversary has been forgotten, but perhaps we need to revisit the chapter on forgiveness. Have we ourselves never forgotten an important remembrance? What's going on in the lives of those people who seem not to be living up to our expectations? And can our expectations be part of the problem?

Our words can wound.

And when they do, we are not only hurting another, we are hurting ourselves as well. Studies today tell us that negativity gets stored in the body. Negativity we receive in the form of criticism directed at us and negativity in the form of criticism we send out to others does indeed have a negative impact on our physical body. Our aches and pains, and other chronic conditions are often very directly connected to the amount of negativity in our environment. Check out *Anatomy of the Spirit* by Carolyn Maas for more information on this concept.

And besides what we are doing to our bodies, of course, we are at risk of losing a possibly very enriching relationship when we are not careful about the words we use when speaking to another. It seems that so many of us are one extreme or the other when it comes to dealing with people. Either we are so afraid of hurting someone that we don't stand up for ourselves, or we are so determined to not be "taken" in any way, that we are not careful about our choice of words when we do stand up for ourselves. Those of us in the second category fail to do enough thinking about the damage words can cause. And it is not just the use of particular words; it is being sensitive to what is going on in people's lives. *Timing is important when we need to confront someone.* If we know that right now the person is having many difficulties in his own life, we may want to wait before we confront. Or, if waiting would not be helpful, we need to be especially careful in the choice of our words.

Let me give you an example. In the church I go to a friend told me of this situation. A month after her mother had died, a woman returned to church, having been out of town attending to the all the details that go with bereavements. On this very first Sunday back, she was accosted by a person who was aware of her mother's death, but who complained about how a certain matter had been handled by the grieving woman several weeks before. You can imagine the result. The relationship between these two people was weakened immeasurably. Timing. It matters.

It's important to keep abreast of people's lives so that we can be sensitive to issues of timing. And that brings up another point. Being an effective communicator takes time. In this day of extreme busyness, it is easy to see why effective communication is so lacking. We have to have the time to pay attention to what is happening in people's lives as well as having the time to think about how to approach them, rather than just blurting out whatever comes first to the tops of our heads.

Exercise: List times you can remember when you wished someone would not have told you some particular thing just at the time that they did. How did you feel?

Recall that feeling whenever you are tempted to jump in with a critical comment for another. Is this the right time? And are these the right words?

How do we ask for things?

Besides having to confront or offer some criticism at times, another difficult communication category is that of asking someone to do something for us. Some of us, unfortunately, do too much ourselves because we are hesitant to ask others for help. This may be because we think only we can do it right — not true, of course. And sometimes we may not want to ask someone to do something because of fear of being turned down.

We need to look at that fear. So what if we are turned down? We don't need to take it personally. Just because someone chooses not to do what we are asking does not mean that we are less valuable as people. It just means the person does not want to do what we are requesting, or perhaps they cannot do it.

Now let's look at how to approach a person when we need to ask for something. When we need to get cooperation from another person, what should we say?

There are two patterns that the majority of people follow, and neither works very well.

1. The first pattern is the dogmatic, "You'll do it because I say so," approach.

While this may get the desired action for a time, eventually the relationship will be ruined if this continues to be the pattern of request.

2. *The second pattern is more subtle.*

And that is its problem. It is so subtle that the person expected to respond doesn't even understand what response is desired. The is the one where the person "hints" at what is wanted by saying things like, "I wish I had more help around the house."

To communicate successfully when cooperation is desired, keep these two principles in mind:

1. Say exactly what it is that is needed.

2. Find a way to lessen the impact this will have on the listener.

Principle number one seems so simple as to be unnecessary but it is proven time and time again that we do not say what we really mean. There are limitless examples. The use of ASAP, for example. When *is* As Soon As Possible? I bet my idea of ASAP is not the same as yours, and in some cases I might get very angry because I wanted something done "as soon as possible," and it seems to be taking forever. Or consider, "when you get a chance." Numerous arguments at work and at home have begun over just such phrases. Or the example in the paragraph above, "I wish I had more help around the house." What help? When? There are so many words which are just too general to let people know clearly what we want. We need to avoid using them.

If we don't know how to express exactly what we want, how can we expect anyone else to know what it is we want?

Many times the source of our not getting what we want is that we don't know exactly what it is ourselves. We may know that we don't like things as they are, but we don't have a concrete enough idea of how to change them to be able to effectively communicate a clear idea to anyone else. So once again it means we must spend some time in our own heads to determine what we will actually be requesting.

What do we mean by ASAP? Do we want the report by Monday? How much time do we mean when we ask our boss for "a little more time" for us to set up the vacation schedule? How much is "some" more money to spend on landscaping? Getting the drift? It is our use of words that are far from specific that can make it very difficult for others to grant our requests.

Some of us mistakenly feel that if we are vague, there will be less chance of confrontation, and that may be true at first. However, sooner or later, usually one party or the other will feel far from satisfied. So, when we are wanting something, it is important to communicate clearly what we want or need. Again, I have to say, we may not get what we are requesting. But at least we will have made our request clear and perhaps opened the door to some negotiation which will come close to satisfying both parties.

The second principle we need to remember is to consider what impact this will have on the listener – that Golden Rule again. That is essential if we are to avoid getting our way by force, perhaps winning the battle, but losing the war. Considering the listener's point of view also greatly increases our chance of success at getting cooperation. No one really likes to be ordered around by anyone. We all know that, and yet when we want our way, we seem to forget that point so easily. When people feel that they have no control, or their point of view is not considered, they have a great reluctance to help; instead they often become defensive and may even try to put up roadblocks.

So, if you have a need that is going to impact on anyone else, it once again takes some creative thinking to determine a way to present this so that the listener doesn't feel his needs are being ignored. If he provides help for us one place, can we provide help for him in another? Or can we find a way to meet our need with very little impact on him?

A great example of this creative communication came from Sarah, a member of one of my earliest workshops. She was in a job that she was not crazy about, but she was having no success in finding another. Because she felt so drained by her unexciting work, she had begun to believe that life was just boring and unfulfilling and that she had no options. After coming to the workshops for a few weeks, she began to see that while she might not be able to change her job right away, she could make some other positive changes in her life that would at least make her non-working hours happier.

Sarah had enjoyed sketching as a young person and was interested in pursuing that, but the class that she really wanted to take was in the daytime, while she was at work. She followed both principles of communication, first deciding exactly what she did want, and then what impact this would have on others. This is the solution she worked out for herself: She asked her boss if she could take off Thursday afternoons to enroll in the sketching class, taking each half day as part of her vacation allowance. He had no objection.

She had done her "homework," and she was successful. While success is not always guaranteed, as we have said, what is guaranteed is that when we consider the other person's needs, as well as our own, we will at least not ruin the relationship. And, if we can't get exactly what we want, perhaps together we can still come up with a viable compromise.

Pete, a person I met at a talk I was doing for a community group, is a marketing manager for a television station. He found he had to work overtime continually to meet all the demands of that position. His health and family life were suffering. Before going to his boss, he analyzed this situation. He saw that all the work needed to be done, but it was just too much for one person. He needed a part-time assistant, but that would cost the station extra money. For some time he had felt there were a couple of ways that money at the station could be saved if certain procedures were changed.

Armed with this information, he went to his boss. Although the boss took a few months to put the proposal into action, in the end Pete got his part-time assistant. The assistant doesn't work for as many hours as Peter had originally wanted; still, as he says, just knowing he had someone else to ease the load gave Pete back his old enthusiasm for the job. He had successfully communicated his needs.

These two principals work in all places with all people. The bottom line is that we all want to feel valued, *all* of us, even the famous and powerful. We stand a much better chance of getting what we need when we remember to consider what effect meeting our goal will have on the others involved.

Once again, I must insert a word of caution here. What happens too often for some people, and especially this can often be true for women, is that we are *so* concerned about the other person we forget what our own needs are. That only leads eventually to feelings of resentment and worse, as we have noted, sometimes to physical and emotional problems. The body does store our pain. We need to remember that we cannot be all things to all people. That is why these two principles are in the order that they are. First we must look to ourselves, to our needs. No one knows us any better than we know ourselves. Then we must look to others.

Recalling again the words of Jesus, "Love your neighbor as you love yourself." We can do it. We must. The world needs people whose lives are working, for themselves, and for the good of everyone. It's our own personal journey, but the results will benefit everyone. May you soon be living enthusiastically and radiating peace.

✠ ✠ ✠

145

About the Author

✠ ✠ ✠

During the six years she spent living in England, Shirley A. Mahood drew on her background as a teacher of English, psychology, and public speaking to develop a series of workshops and seminars on improving our lives. The first edition of this book was published in London.

Headquartered again in the United States, she has continued developing her workshops and seminars, resulting in this new edition of *Making Our Lives Work*.

Personal experience has sharpened her insights and sensitivities towards those who need a new way of looking at daily existence. Her gentle, loving approach envelopes the principles presented here for living a more complete, provident life.

Your comments and suggestions are welcome.

For information about workshops, classes, or lectures, write to

Shirley A. Mahood
e-mail: smahood@cox.net

✠ ✠ ✠